Fortress Britain?

Fortress Britain?

Ethical approaches to immigration
policy for a post-Brexit Britain

Edited by
Ben Ryan

Jessica Kingsley *Publishers*
London and Philadelphia

First published in 2018
by Jessica Kingsley Publishers
73 Collier Street
London N1 9BE, UK
and
400 Market Street, Suite 400
Philadelphia, PA 19106, USA

www.jkp.com

Library of Congress Cataloging in Publication Data
A CIP catalog record for this book is available from the Library of Congress

British Library Cataloguing in Publication Data
A CIP catalogue record for this book is available from the British Library

ISBN 978 1 78592 309 8
eISBN 978 1 78450 620 9

Printed and bound in Great Britain

MIX
Paper from
responsible sources
FSC® C013056

Contents

Introduction

Ben Ryan, Theos Think Tank

Why this book?

Immigration has been a critical issue in UK politics for decades. In the 1940s and 1950s the debate centred on the British Nationality Act that granted British citizenship to Commonwealth citizens and the subsequent 'Windrush', as West Indian migrants entered the UK. In the 1960s it was the Race Relations Act, and Enoch Powell's infamous 'Rivers of Blood' speech that sparked debate and confrontation. Tony Blair's efforts to introduce multiculturalism and the European Union's commitment to the free movement of people provided further challenges in the 1990s and 2000s. The challenges of integration are longstanding – whether of the Irish, West Indian or more recent Muslim populations.

The EU referendum of 2016 brought many of these decades-old clashes to a head. Although the vote was strictly concerning the UK's membership of the EU, in practice it became a battle between a 'Remain' campaign fixated on economics and a 'Leave' campaign that put considerable weight on the issue of migration. Both sides had other strings to their bows. It would be absurd to claim that every Remain supporter did so for the sake of national GDP, or that every Leave voter was only concerned with immigration. However, as a broad categorisation, that clash of campaigns holds up.

In fact, even beyond the spectre of a European debate, those two sides reveal something of the mess that has come to define the UK approach towards migration. Incompatible value structures lead to policies that oscillate wildly in their ultimate goal. On the one hand, migrants are tolerated (even at times encouraged) as 'economic units' who can further the British economic machine. On the other, they are perceived as a threat, representing the dilution and undermining of the British sense of national identity. One group sees migrants as essential to a bright economic future. Another (sometimes overlapping) group sees migrants as good for British culture; providing new cuisines, new music, new traditions and a new, brighter, more cosmopolitan nation. Another group perceives the effects of migration as undermining community – they say they do not recognise their own country any more, and that they want what they had back. Some see migrants as a threat to their safety, in terms of international terrorism.

In this context of competing value structures, and policies that reflect one approach under particular governments only to be subsequently reversed by another, Brexit provides a new horizon. The UK will, at some point in the relatively near future, cease to be part of the EU. It will then have the opportunity to start from scratch, to consider its migration policy and decide just what it wants to embody.

This opportunity provides space for critical reflection. Before enacting a new migration policy, now is the time to ask: what will be the values that will inform what we, as a nation, choose to do next? What ethical values make the best basis for making a coherent and consistent approach to migration?

Why draw on Christian ethics for this collection?

In searching for a new ethical basis to migration, this collection draws from Christian ethical concerns in particular. Undoubtedly, there are other ethical models on which a response could be drawn, and this is not an attempt to claim that there is only one basis on which it would be possible to proceed. As will become clear, although the contributions of this volume draw on Christian ethics, the particular aspects of that tradition on which they choose to draw vary considerably, as do the conclusions they draw from their approach. The point of this collection was to open up a new discussion on the basis for migration policy. These contributions are one aspect of that conversation.

Beyond that, however, there are good reasons for taking a particularly Christian approach seriously on these issues. For one thing, Christianity provides a language in which the British and the migrant communities can converse. For the former, although fewer than ever before now self-identify as Christian (the most recent British Social Attitudes survey found that 53 per cent of British adults now have no religion and only 41 per cent are Christian[1]), the UK remains a place shaped and defined by its Christian history and values.

In an institutional sense this can be linked to the established Church of England, with its constitutional status that guarantees a level of political and public presence. However, more significant is a cultural sense in which, even without high levels of belief, the UK is still defined by a Christian intellectual values structure in some way. Jean-Paul Sartre was discussing the Europe of the 1970s when he declared that,

> ...we are all still Christians today; the most radical unbelief is Christian atheism, an atheism that despite its destructive power preserves guiding schemes - very few for thought, more for the imagination, most for the sensibility, whose source lies in the centuries of Christianity to which we are heirs, like it or not.[2]

Less polemically, we might describe the UK of today as being in a state of 'belonging but not believing', to flip the famous formula of the British sociologist Grace Davie.[3] In this sense the UK has become a space which culturally identifies with Christianity, and is informed by it, even if increasingly few people attend church or believe in God.

As for migrants, they are significantly more likely to be religious (and Christian) than the British. Migrants into the UK are more than three times more likely than natives to attend a religious service weekly, or to pray daily.[4] The 2011 Census revealed that just under 50 per cent of the non-UK-born population self-identified as Christian, 19 per cent as Muslim, while only 15 per cent had no religion.[5] In searching for a shared register, therefore, religion in general (and Christianity in particular) has much to recommend it. For both the British indigenous population and migrant communities, an ethical model from within Christianity connects well with their own identities. For those fearing that their identity could be fatally undermined by migration (either because they feel they are being replaced, or that assimilation will compromise their own beliefs and traditions) having a value structure that speaks in a religious language would be a valuable asset.

A second reason to take Christian ethics seriously in this field is that Christians have earned the right to have a voice in a sector in which they play a major role. Particularly when it comes to work with refugees, Christian charities and interventions seem to take on a disproportionate scale of the work. Among the Christian operations in this space are the City of Sanctuary movement, community sponsorship schemes, the For Refugees group, the Boaz Trust and many others. Anna Rowlands' chapter below draws on the experience of one such group (the Jesuit Refugee Service). Given the scale of activity being undertaken by Christian groups it seems appropriate to engage with their ethical reasoning.

Finally, this collection looks at Christian ethics because there is rich material on which to draw. Christianity and Judaism have much to offer on theories of migration. As Susanna Snyder's chapter shows, there is a great deal of material on the experience of travelling and migration – to the extent that there is a case to be made that migration defines something of the human condition. Much of the Old Testament is explicitly concerned with the experience of the Jewish people and their patriarchs travelling from one place to another, or finding themselves in exile away from their home.

The New Testament too finds Jesus and then his followers travelling and spreading the gospel ever wider across the Mediterranean world. The early experience of Christians was of a minority faith in a hostile environment, subverting many of the norms of the Roman world by denying that their religion was tied to a particular ethnic group.

Alongside this material on the experience of migration, Christian political theology has also developed a sophisticated conception of the nation, and what it means to be part of the nation (the Western model of nationhood, in fact, owes much to the Old Testament model of Israel). This too provides a useful lens through which to construct an ethical approach to migration, since the nation as a locus of identity is one of the key features in debates over citizenship and fears of cultural takeover.

Putting those together with the broader Christian theological traditions around the use of power and government, and the treatment of outsiders, and there are the makings of a fairly comprehensive body of thought on which to base a migration policy.

For all these reasons, the authenticity of an approach which speaks to British cultural belonging and migrant faith, the scope of current Christian activity in this space and the depth of the intellectual reservoir that Christian theology can provide, Christian ethics are an excellent source on which to build a new, ethical approach to migration policy.

How the collection works

The chapters in this collection are not designed to provide consensus on complex policy issues, but to provoke a new conversation around the basis on which we establish a migration policy. Each contribution challenges something of our current settlement on migration with an ethical call to enact something different, grounded in a clear new basis.

The contributions are broadly divided into two sets. The first three chapters take a broad view of migration, making a case for how we ought to establish the right to migrate into the UK, and what voices and ideas ought to underpin that policy. They represent a varied approach to that issue.

Adrian Pabst's chapter suggests a model based on virtue and the common good, which recognises that humans are neither simply individual, autonomous agents, nor commodified labour, but operate in relationships. His model proposes policy recommendations that avoid the trap of seeing migrants as either a matter of economic utility, or migrations simply as a matter of personal freedom.

My own chapter proposes a policy for the UK that prioritises an international rights model. This would start from the recognition of human dignity and ward against the danger of state interests coming to view migrants as dehumanised commodities, or threats. It suggests a need for a stronger international rights framework to prevent the abuse of the system by competing state interests.

David Goodhart takes a very different approach. His proposals are based on the need to support national solidarity and reduce the rapid ethnic change that can, he argues, undermine social cohesion and public confidence, while maintaining the economic benefits that migration can provide. He also raises the spectre of the need for international solidarity, and the prevention of a 'brain drain' from poorer countries to the West.

The other four chapters look at the issue of the integration and treatment of migrants once they have arrived in the UK.

Unlike the first four, which look at migration policy in terms of how to assess people coming in, they look at the situation of people already present within the UK and how policy ought to affect the treatment of those migrants.

Anna Rowlands considers the particular experience of asylum seekers attempting to navigate a policy world in which there is now the 'systematic deployment of destitution and detention as forms of border management'. She argues that the current political approaches to asylum have forgotten that the task of politics is to enact the good and restrain evil.

Pia Jolliffe and Samuel Burke look at the particular issues around child migration. Based on interviews with politicians, aid workers and volunteers, this chapter draws attention to child migrants' vulnerability due to their legal status, conditions of their country of origin, gender, ethnicity, religious affiliation and social status. The chapter also looks at the impact of the recent Dubs Amendment and criticizes the government for failing in its responsibilities.

Mohammed Girma offers a broader view of integrating different migrant communities. Rejecting past multicultural efforts as unsatisfactory, he instead argues for 'narrative reasoning' as a better means of creating mutual understanding and long-term social cohesion, since it would counteract the current fear of diversity and fit the internal logic of Judaeo-Christian notions of community.

Susanna Snyder also engages with the theme of interaction between the host community and migrants. She argues that the Bible gives us a model in which humanity is in a constant state of migration, and yet seeking a settled home. She presents a case for seeing the key to strengthening culture, given that model of humanity, not in isolation but in a mutually empowering encounter.

As the summaries here make clear, these chapters coalesce around a theme: proposing a new ethical core with which to assess migration policy. They are not designed to be in agreement with one another, nor do they necessarily address the same aspects of a large and complex policy area.

This collection is not intended to be a manifesto or policy brief, but to provoke much-needed discussion on the question of what values will shape the UK's approach to migration in the future, and how particular values might shape policy. The Brexit process provides arguably the single most significant opportunity for a fundamental review of what the UK wants to be, and how it wishes to act on the world stage, since the end of the Second World War. Migration is a critical part of that debate, and it is hoped that these essays will provide a spur for that discussion.

Facts and statistics: the current context

Before turning to the essays themselves, it is worth briefly outlining the current state of migration (as of late 2017) in the UK. Despite – or perhaps because of – the prominence of immigration in public debates, there is a lot of misinformation and confusion regarding the current situation. A 2016 poll by Ipsos Mori found that British people greatly over-estimate how many EU migrants are in the UK: on average, they thought EU citizens make up 15 per cent of the total UK population, when in reality it's 5 per cent.[6] This was in line with a series of polls[7] carried out by multiple bodies which have consistently shown that the British over-estimate the numbers of immigrants present in the UK.

This underlines the extent to which the public narrative has focused on immigration as a problematic issue. However, although the British public are largely wrong on how much migration there is into the UK, it would be nonsense to therefore dismiss all the fears associated with migration. There a significant level of migration into the UK and there are real challenges for integration and, in places, public services.

Nevertheless, forming judgements and policy based on major misconceptions is dangerous and, in that spirit, the current context of migration into the UK (and internationally) is presented below.

Unless explicitly stated otherwise all the following data are drawn from the Office for National Statistics (ONS) Migration Statistics Quarterly Report: August 2017.[8]

- In total, for the year ending March 2017, total immigration to the UK was 588,000. This was about 50,000 fewer than the previous year.
- Of that total, 275,000 (or a little under 50 per cent of the total) immigrated to work in the UK, 188,000 (just under 70 per cent) of them with a definite job.
- In the same period, there were 16,211 people granted asylum, resettlement or an alternative form of protection. That equates to around 3 per cent of total immigration.
- Long-term immigration to study (students) was 139,000 for the same period – a drop of 27,000 on the previous year.
- At the same time, total emigration from the UK was 342,000. This was an increase of 31,000 on the previous year.
- Net migration (the total figure reached by finding the difference between immigration and emigration) to the UK was therefore 246,000, a significant 81,000 fewer than the previous year. This change was driven largely by a significant increase in emigration from the UK by EU citizens, particularly those from the EU8 (Czech Republic, Estonia, Hungary, Latvia, Lithuania, Poland, Slovakia and Slovenia).
- Total migration from the EU was around 248,000, a significant drop on the previous year. Total migration from non-EU countries came to 266,000. The number of British citizens migrating into the UK from abroad was 74,000.
- The reasons for moving vary considerably between EU migrants, non-EU migrants and returning British citizens:
    - Of EU citizens, around 70 per cent move for work, with the majority of those having a definite job offer.

Only around 10 per cent move to accompany or join others (e.g. migrating to join family, migrating in order to marry and so on).

- Of non-EU citizens, over 40 per cent are students moving for study and 21 per cent are moving to accompany or join others.

• In total, there are now 9.2 million people resident in the UK who were born abroad. Of those, the largest single groups are Poles (911,000), Indians (833,000), Pakistanis (534,000), Irish (389,000) and Romanians (310,000).[9]

• There is significant regional variance when it comes to the density of non-UK-born residents in a given area. The local authority with the highest proportion of non-British nationals is Kensington and Chelsea at 37 per cent. There are six London local authorities that have a proportion of non-British nationals above 30 per cent (no local authorities outside of London exceed 30 per cent). By contrast, Nah-Eileanan an Iar (the Western Isles of Scotland) is, rather unsurprisingly, 0 per cent, and only four Welsh local authorities exceed 5 per cent.[10]

• Non-EU migration is assessed according to a points-based system that divides migrants into five tiers:

- Tier 1 is for 'high value migrants', including investors, entrepreneurs and those deemed an 'exceptional talent'.
- Tier 2 is for skilled workers with a UK job offer. This includes transfers within international companies and skilled workers in sectors with a proven shortage.
- Tier 3 has been indefinitely suspended and has never been used, but was designed for low-skilled workers in sectors with a temporary shortage. Membership of the EU has, in practice, meant that there has never been such a shortage, though it is possible to envisage that changing post-Brexit.
- Tier 4 is for students who have secured a place at a registered British educational establishment.

- Tier 5 is a temporary worker category that includes sub-categories including for young people on gap years with countries operating a reciprocal relationship, sportspeople and athletes, charity workers and others.
- A separate system covers family visas, for people looking to join family within the UK.
- Internationally, the UN report of 2015 put the total number of migrants worldwide at 244 million, up from the previous high of 222 million in 2010, and from 173 million in 2000.[11] That included around 20 million refugees.
- More than half (53 per cent) of all refugees worldwide came from just three countries: the Syrian Arab Republic, Afghanistan and Somalia.[12]

This provides the essential context behind any discussion of migration. It is important to differentiate between UK migration (which fell last year), and the international context. Worldwide migration is increasingly common. In both the UK and internationally, only a relatively small portion of migrants are refugees (although the number of refugees is increasing and, of course, their needs are significantly greater than those of other migrant groups).

With that context established, we can now turn to the contributions themselves.

ENDNOTES

1. Press release from the National Centre for Social Research. 'British Social Attitudes: Record number of Brits with no religion.' 4 September 2017, Accessed 21 September 2017 at http://www.natcen.ac.uk/news-media/press-releases/2017/september/british-social-attitudes-record-number-of-brits-with-no-religion

2. Sartre, J. (1991) *The Family Idiot*. Chicago: Chicago University Press, p.346.

3. Davie, G. (1994) *Religion in Britain Since 1945: Believing Without Belonging*. Oxford: Blackwell.

4. van Tubrergen, F. and Sindradóttir, J.Í. (2011) 'The Religiosity of Immigrants in Europe: A Cross-National Study.' *Journal for the Scientific Study of Religion*, 50, 2, 272–88.

5. Census 2011. A summary is provided by the Office for National Statistics '2011 Census analysis: Ethnicity and religion of the non-UK born population in England and Wales: 2011', 18 June, 2015.

6. Ipsos Mori. (2016) 'The perils of perception and the EU.' Accessed 21 September 2017 at https://www.ipsos.com/ipsos-mori/en-uk/perils-perception-and-eu

7. Ipsos Mori. (2013) 'Perceptions are not reality.' Accessed 30 November 2017 at https://www.kcl.ac.uk/newsevents/news/newsrecords/2013/07-July/Perceptions-are-not-reality-the-top-10-we-get-wrong.aspx

8. Office for National Statistics. 'Migration Statistics Quarterly Report: 24 August 2017.' Accessed 15 September 2017 at https://www.ons.gov.uk/peoplepopulationandcommunity/populationandmigration/internationalmigration/bulletins/migrationstatisticsquarterlyreport/august2017

9. ONS. (2017) 'Population of the UK by country of birth and nationality: 2016.' Statistical bulletin, 24 August 2017. Accessed 15 September 2017 at https://www.ons.gov.uk/peoplepopulationandcommunity/populationandmigration/internationalmigration/bulletins/ukpopulationbycountryofbirthandnationality/2016

10. Ibid.

11. United Nations. (2016) 'International Migration Report 2015'.

12. Ibid.

1

Mutual Obligations

A Common Good Approach to Immigration[1]

Adrian Pabst, University of Kent

Reframing the debate on immigration

The debate on immigration has been dominated by economic or political considerations that rest on utilitarian or deontological principles. Indeed, the case for immigration is generally couched in abstract terms of the overall, aggregate impact, or the freedom of movement as a fundamental right. However, appeals to material utility and personal liberty ring hollow, because such ideals too often overlook the relationships with our family, friends, colleagues, fellow citizens or strangers (who can also be our new neighbours), which provide substance to otherwise vacuous values. These approaches focus on the individual and the collective, at the expense of all the intermediate groups and communities that constitute society.

By contrast, an approach centred on virtue involves judgement about how the common good should be pursued in the public sphere and what the policy and institutional arrangements might be that enable citizens and migrants to lead a good life. Such an approach focuses on the implications of migration, not just for host countries, but also for 'sending countries'. In particular, the importance of mutual regard, i.e. a disposition of reciprocal sacrifice that underpins the willingness to cooperate and share risks, resources and rewards.

One key issue is the volume of emigration and immigration, and the sheer rate of change for all people involved, which can undermine the social fabric in the countries of origin and of destination. Thus, a public philosophy of the common good shifts the emphasis away from the individual or the collective to the relational – the mutual obligations that beget rights and create the conditions for human flourishing.

Catholic Social Thought and cognate traditions in other Christian churches emphasise the importance of reciprocity in addition to compassion: Pope Francis puts this well. He has called on states and citizens not only to welcome refugees who face persecution or extreme economic hardship but also to provide assistance to countries whence migrants originate in order to allow people to stay at home: 'The Church stands at the side of all who work to defend each person's right to live with dignity, first and foremost by exercising the right not to emigrate and to contribute to the development of one's country of origin.'[2]

This essay argues that Christian social teaching provides conceptual and practical resources to reframe the debate about immigration. This issue is not simply a matter of policy but of political philosophy and theology. Immigration raises questions about the balance between the rights of immigrants and the legitimate concerns of citizens in host countries about their national identity, as well as about the mutual obligation to foster integration into adopted societies.[3] These are questions of justice – a philosophy of how we should treat one another, how the law should be and how interpersonal relations in society should be organised.[4] The Christian tradition makes a unique contribution to public debate and policy as it seeks to transcend the opposition that pits egotism against altruism by trying to hold in balance self-love and love of the other. This obligation is linked to the preferential option for the poor – to help the poor, vulnerable and voiceless to become active participants in society, so that all may share in and contribute to the common good.

A concern for justice is not a pious demand for more morality in public life, as if ethics were something alien to politics and in tension with its more pragmatic and realistic requirements. Instead, politics is concerned with justice, and so it is always already intertwined with ethics. But competing conceptions of justice hold radically different answers to questions about whether politics ought to be concerned with what is a flourishing society and with how we lead a lead a worthy human existence and a rewarding life. The real issue is therefore about the teleology or purpose of politics – what is good or desirable as an end to be pursued and achieved?

Especially in times of division, there is a strong desire for shared purpose. In her maiden speech in the House of Commons, the MP Jo Cox (who was murdered in June 2016) put this well: 'we are far more united and have far more in common with each other than things that divide us'.[5]

How can politics and public policy reflect this quest? Drawing on Christian social teaching, this essay sets out an approach to immigration based on a conception of justice that is centred on virtue, the common good and the dignity of the person.

Virtue is a habit or quality that enables human beings to pursue their purpose, which is to lead a good life. A good life combines individual fulfilment with mutual flourishing in association with others – fulfilling the unique talents of each and pursuing the common good of all. The common good is not a simple sum of individual goods, like total national output, but rather all the goods that only exist in the act of sharing them – trust, friendship and all the relationships of cooperation that give meaning to our activities.[6] This involves seeing our fundamental identity beyond our individual selves and making personal sacrifices so that the shared identity may be affirmed and strengthened. Another way of saying this is to suggest that society is a covenant between generations that balances freedom and autonomy with solidarity and care for others. A society that reflects our social, relational nature rejects the cult of rampant individualism and arbitrary restrictions on freedom that come with the cult of nationalism.

Immigration and rival conceptions of justice

In Britain, free movement of people as part of EU membership, as well as the ongoing refugee emergency in Syria and growing levels of migration from parts of Africa and Asia, have put immigration front and centre of public debate. A lot of the current political discussion revolves around finding a simple policy fix to address these problems. But, in order to develop a plausible and constructive alternative to the current situation, what is required is a different approach that does not accept the assumptions on which the dominant models of political economy rest, starting with the conception of the person as an isolated individual who seeks to maximise either utility or freedom of choice.

The backlash against the impact of globalisation on countries and communities raises fundamental questions about the assumptions that underpin the two dominant models of political economy over the past half-century. First, the post-war settlement of 'embedded liberalism' that was regulated by Keynesian economics of full employment and demand management. Second, the post-1970s settlement of 'neo-liberalism' that was driven by Hayekian economics of controlling inflation and enacting supply-side reforms. Both models viewed state and market as the key institutions to govern society: whereas the first focused on the administrative state to control from the top down hitherto more mutual arrangements, the second shifted the emphasis to the free market as the main mode of social organisation.[7]

Whatever their important ideological and policy differences, both models assume that people seek to maximise utility and individual freedom of choice. Both models also assume that in the economy human beings are essentially isolated individuals who contract with one another in pursuit of their self-interested personal preferences. And both assume that, in the global marketplace, people have a price and can be traded like commodities.

But from the perspective of Christian social teaching and cognate traditions, human beings are, primarily, social beings who are constituted by relationships, not transactions, and who are engaged with others in pursuit of meaning. Such an anthropology suggests that people want to realise their potential, flourish in association with fellow human beings and lead rewarding lives.[8] This includes accumulating and consuming wealth, but it extends to a sense of caring, earning and belonging. People care for family, friends, colleagues, neighbours and also strangers in their midst. They want to earn an income in order to feed themselves and their loved ones, but they equally want to earn respect and recognition for who they are and for what they contribute to community and country. People want to belong to particular places, and they search for some measure of stability and a role in society.[9]

There is therefore a tension between more freely roaming capital on the one hand, and people who tend to favour settled over nomadic ways of life on the other hand. The free movement of capital is at odds with the free movement of people in a way that is not the case for the cross-border circulation of goods and services, as capital is a major pull factor for migrants. But just as migration flows and capital movements are international, so too the backlash against globalisation in the Brexit and Trump vote suggests that a sizeable part of the electorate do not want their national government to lose control over immigration or the national economy. In each case, concerns about the legitimacy of decision-making and a lack of democratic accountability raise fundamental questions about the nature of state and market institutions. Ultimately some public authority has to have the final say over managing migration and capital flows – either national government or a supranational body.

Both in Christian social teaching and in the EU treaties, this question is addressed in terms of the principle of subsidiarity. The prevailing conception of subsidiarity is formal and therefore focuses on the functional level of decision-making, but this brackets substantive issues out of the question – what is the purpose of locating sovereign power at different levels? Is it the maximisation of utility or freedom of choice? Or is the purpose mutual flourishing in association with others and in line with both the common good and the dignity of the person? These are questions of justice that are central to a richer political debate and better public policy making. Three conceptions of justice can be distinguished:

1. Maximising utility, defined as 'the greatest happiness of the greatest number'.
2. Expanding freedom, defined in terms of individual liberties and rights.
3. Promoting virtue and the common good, defined as the 'greatest good for all people' linked to human dignity and the holistic fulfilment of people as part of communities of true persons.

The first approach draws on the utilitarian philosophy of Jeremy Bentham and others, and it views the maximisation of utility as the main measure of justice. Utility can take the form of private happiness or collective wellbeing judged, for example, by some aggregate measure such as GDP, but the point is that utility deals with totals rather distribution.

The second approach focuses on freedom. It considers the respect for individual liberties and rights as the best means of attaining justice. Freedom tends to be conceived as the absence of constraints on people except for the law and private conscience rather than the freedom to pursue a particular end.

The third approach emphasises the promotion of virtue which, in the tradition of Aristotle and many Christian thinkers, means the human capacity to do good and pursue the goods inherent in each activity: being a good parent, neighbour, employee, business owner or fellow citizen. This model views justice in terms of the common good, defined as the good of each and every one of us as we concretely are in our families, workplaces, communities, nations and beyond.

Models of justice based on utility and freedom can make a valuable contribution to the debate on immigration. The notion of utility is key to understanding the costs and benefits of immigration for 'sending' and host countries. The notion of freedom is central to the choice of individuals as they seek to improve their own conditions and those of others. However, both these conceptions of justice are limited. Neither approach has much to say about what binds us together as social beings. Both are silent on what constitutes the good life. Instead, the assumption is that this is for everyone to decide individually, and not in association with others – let alone as part of a community within or beyond the nation. Therefore both models exclude from the court of public discussion questions about shared purposes or ends that can bind people together and shape the actions of persons or groups.

Virtue and the common good

An approach to justice based on virtue and the common good can enrich notions of utility and freedom and also complement them. Broadly speaking, virtue means the human capacity to do good and to pursue the goods that are specific to each activity – being a good parent, neighbour, employee, business owner or fellow citizen. This can perhaps best be understood as a mode of personal fulfilment and mutual flourishing. It seeks to fulfil one's character and to pursue purposes that are internal to human action in cooperation with others based on shared ends. To be virtuous is to perform well by fulfilling a certain goal. So the question is not what we should do faced with such and such a predicament, but rather what should we consistently be doing . What sort of character do we want to be and how should we order this desire in an acceptable way to our relationships with others?

By emphasising notions of goodness and purpose, a focus on virtue differs fundamentally from approaches to justice that focus on maximising individual happiness, collective utility, personal freedoms or rights. Virtue offers a more holistic perspective that is not limited to purely instrumental value but extends to shared ends or finalities. In this manner, virtue shifts the emphasis from regulating behaviour to fostering character. Virtue is not about moral codes of conduct, or externally imposed rules and regulations. Rather, virtue marks the development of good habits through practice in collaboration with a supportive community based upon shared values.

At the heart of virtue are notions of excellence and ethos – that people can reach their highest human potential and do so in ways that promote the flourishing of others too. This can be achieved with a different set of institutions and practices that provide incentives and rewards for virtuous behaviour. It is in human flourishing and pursuing the good life that the complete expression of human potential for excellence is realised.

Central to the pursuit of a good life are the virtues that define the character of a person. Character connects knowledge and skills to judgement. To foster character is to help people develop the ability to do 'the right thing' in response to dilemmas. However, this is less about problem-solving and more about what Aristotle called 'practical wisdom' (*phronesis*) – linking our motivations and values to purpose and the right course of action. In short, virtue promotes 'good-doing' rather than 'do-gooding', and it tries to help achieve wider ends by serving the needs and interests of individuals and society – the common good.

The common good can be described as the good of each and every one of us as we concretely are in our families, workplaces, communities, nations and beyond. The Catholic Christian tradition has bequeathed to us a rich conception of the common good. According to the Second Vatican Council:

The common good is the sum of those conditions of social life, which allow social groups and their individual members relatively thorough and ready access to their own fulfilment. The common good also provides a balance against too strong an individualism by emphasising the social aspect of the human person. Authentic development is possible only if an individual interacts with and grows within a society. Thus each of us is required to work for the common good which includes all others within society. Even property of its nature also has a social aspect, which is based on the law of the common purpose of goods.[10]

Catholic Social Thought also provides a helpful definition:

The common good does not consist in the simple sum of the particular goods of each subject of a social entity. Belonging to everyone and to each person, it is and remains 'common' because it is indivisible and because only together it is possible to attain it, increase it and safeguard its effectiveness.[11]

This definition suggests that there are three key components: first, the common good is not a sum total; second, the common good is indivisible; third, sharing in the common good and contributing to it is a joint activity, not an individual action. Therefore a common good approach to justice differs from the impersonal justice of the utility-based model and the individualistic justice of the rights-based model by emphasising that justice is relational – the right ordering of relations in society.

The common good includes all the goods we hold jointly, such as friendship, trust and 'social capital', i.e. networks of interpersonal relationships among people who live and work together. Such goods are relational and non-material, but they affect the production, exchange and enjoyment of material goods – whether momentarily with strangers or continuously with friends, colleagues or fellow citizens.[12] For example, economic transactions characterised by greater reciprocity and a balance of interests can improve the efficiency of business transactions and make them more robust. In short, a more just economy can also be a more productive and efficient economy.[13]

So defined, virtue and the common good encompass both individual fulfilment (the unique talents and vocations of each and every one) and mutual flourishing (the balance between personal autonomy and dependence on others).

In summary: appeals to utility and individual freedom are important, but they can ring hollow because such principles too often overlook the relationships with our family, friends, colleagues, fellow citizens or strangers, which provide substance to otherwise vacuous values. By contrast, a focus on virtue involves judgement about how the common good should be pursued in the public sphere and what policy and institutional arrangements might be available that enable citizens to live a good life. Such questions are central to a sense of justice and fair play.

A common good approach to immigration

A common good approach to immigration has to begin with the recognition that people are not commodities. Refugees, as a particular category of migrant, should not be viewed as anonymous and deracinated economic agents, uprooted from their linguistic, familial, cultural and religious hinterland. Rather, most if not all refugees are deeply invested in their identities and they long to be recognised within a host country with its political system and culture. And those who wish to return eventually to their countries of origin do not seek a nomadic existence elsewhere and do not want their families to be rootless. The point is that the mobility of people has to have limits, which go beyond considerations of utility or freedom because people are embedded in social and cultural ties – even though they should not be constrained by them. If they are not commodities, then they must have intrinsic worth and a wider purpose. Therefore it is the reasoned and purposeful movement of people that needs to be considered.

In turn, this means that an approach to immigration has to be concerned with more than utility or liberty. An approach focused on the ethics of virtue and the common good would make distinctions between different kinds of migration. In terms of migration, this would need to be looked at from the perspective of both the freedom and dignity of the individual and the impact of his or her movement on others. There is a case to strengthen the distinction between refugees who flee war and escape persecution, and migrants who leave behind deprivation and are in search of better opportunities for themselves and their families. While the plight of refugees is a humanitarian catastrophe, the situation of many economic migrants is dire but not as desperate. And while stable and prosperous societies have a moral duty to welcome the former and provide them with proper help (not least because countries contribute to migration through their foreign policy, arms sales, etc.), they do not have the same obligation to accept migrants.

The quest for human flourishing is clearly not the same as self-interest and individual advancement. It implies a sense of obligations to others and their flourishing too, as both depend on one another. Obligations involve loyalty and sympathy with the people around us – family, neighbours, colleagues, fellow citizens and people from elsewhere. Indeed, the strangers in our midst can be our neighbours. At the same time, not all men and women have an equal claim to people's affections. Christ's injunction to love our neighbour as ourselves does of course extend to the stranger, but it does not abolish the importance of kin, tribe and nation, and the interpersonal relationships of reciprocity.

From this perspective, borders should never been seen as absolute or confined to the territorial boundaries of sovereign states. A sense of community and shared 'social imaginary' (Charles Taylor's famous term[14]) often extends across national frontiers – especially in the case of Europe and its ties to other countries (much more so than, say, Japan). At the same time, borders matter to people's identity and therefore cannot be seen as entirely arbitrary either. In the Christian tradition, there is a balance between belonging to particular places and people on the one hand, and belonging to a universal human community, on the other hand.

Here it is instructive to draw on the tradition of virtue ethics that we owe to the fusion of Greco-Roman philosophy (the four classical virtues) with biblical revelation (the three theological virtues), notably Aristotle's idea of the 'radical' middle way that charts an alternative to the excess of a characteristic associated with a virtue (too much courage leads to recklessness) or a deficiency in virtue (too little courage entails cowardice). Applied to the question of immigration, the middle way is between, on the one hand, xenophobia, chauvinism, discrimination and nationalism, and on the other hand a lack of regard for one's own country and its people and the privileging of foreigners over fellow citizens. Put differently, we need an alternative to both egotism and altruism because neither is relational and both fail to practice the principle of reciprocity or gift-exchange.

Francis' position is a case in point. He has urged states and citizens not only to welcome refugees who face persecution or extreme economic hardship but also to provide assistance to countries whence migrants originate in order to allow people to stay at home:

> *The Church stands at the side of all who work to defend each person's right to live with dignity, first and foremost by exercising the right not to emigrate and to contribute to the development of one's country of origin.*[15]

Beyond the choice between an open- and a closed-door policy for people or money, Christian social teaching reminds us that mercy and compassion have to be combined with assistance for people in their own countries and programmes of integration that take into account the rights and duties of all – indigenous people and migrants alike, or business owners and workers. Developing and increasing assistance so that conditions in home countries improve is the best discouragement to mass migration, but many people who want to cut immigration also want to cut foreign aid. By the same token, a migration impact fund might be part of a wider recognition that host countries face economic challenges in welcoming migrants, and that the cultural impact of the volume and pace of migration also needs to be taken into much greater account.

In summary, a common good approach tries to take a more holistic approach to the free movement of capital and people. Beyond utility and freedom, this approach rejects the idea that money and migrants are mere commodities and instead views them in more relational terms and as having intrinsic worth or value.

Some public policy ideas based on a common good approach

A common good approach rests on three principles that frame policy ideas.

First, the principle of subsidiarity, which means taking decisions on the free movement of people and capital at the most appropriate level in line with the dignity of the person and the dignity of work. In practice, this means working out where international cooperation is the right place for decision, when it is the national level and when it is the regional or local level. Even more important than the level of action is, first, the balance of interest and, second, the distribution of power between different authorities and institutions.

Second, the principle of solidarity, which focuses on the importance of interpersonal relationships and the role of fraternity or fellowship in making and implementing decisions. In practice, this requires two things: a greater attention to virtuous leadership – thought leaders and decision-makers leading by example; and popular participation – more involvement of people where they are in their communities and professions.

Third, the principle of reciprocity or give-and-take, which shifts the emphasis to the importance of honouring the contribution people can make to society – whether through work, providing care (children or the elderly) or in other ways. In practice, this means a greater balance of interests between different sections of society in neighbourhoods, communities, professions, (e.g. by reforming the governance arrangements of businesses, trade unions, local government, the civil service, etc.).

These three principles translate into a primacy of society over politics and the economy, i.e. the primacy of intermediary institutions where personhood and community can be worked out. The Church, alongside faith communities and civil society organisations, could and should play a greater role to help direct government and business towards interpersonal solutions that contribute to the common good.

We have to switch focus away from administrative procedure and policy process to the shaping of character, the nurturing of behaviour and the building of institutions that are not subject to short-term party political pressure but reflect the longer-term national interest. Possibilities include not just establishing Royal Commissions (and Royal Colleges for vocations that are currently not represented) but also a Church-led national dialogue in association with people of all faiths and none.

Taken as a whole, an approach might reflect the following policy ideas:

Providing sanctuary and hospital treatment for refugees
- Improve access to the system for those seeking sanctuary from war or persecution, which involves differentiating those seeking sanctuary from other migrants (in particular economic migration).
- Create a better 'protection culture' for those seeking sanctuary (including better access to legal advice and representation, a faster appeals process).
- Offer fair and humane treatment for those being granted sanctuary (including access to housing, public services and English-language classes, as well as work for those who can make a contribution).

- Recognise the particular plight of certain groups, (e.g. Yazidi, Christians, or Sufi Muslims in Iraq and Syria), and provide targeted help (including access to religious books and facilities for worship in refugee camps).
- Increase the number of unaccompanied children allowed into the UK and other developed countries.
- Increase the number of refugees via the Syria Vulnerable Person Resettlement Programme.

Restricting the volume of economic migration

- Help migrants where they are – not just in their own countries through more targeted trade and development policy but also those fleeing deprivation in the regions (not refugee camps with tents but pre-fabricated villages with better facilities).
- Facilitate the entry of migrants who study or have been offered employment, but limit the stay of those in search of employment to shorter periods.
- Introduce where so far absent a legal obligation to register with local government in order to keep track of newly arrived migrants.
- Facilitate access to public services for those in situations of hardship, but limit access to certain public services such as social housing to those in employment until they have contributed for some time.

ENDNOTES

1. This chapter draws on an essay entitled 'Reforming free movement of people and capital: a common good approach' (London: St Paul's Institute, March 2018).
2. Pope Francis. (2016) 'Message for the World: Day of Migrants and Refugees 2016' The Vatican, 17 January 2016.
3. Miller, D. (2016) *Strangers in Our Midst: The Political Philosophy of Immigration.* Cambridge, MA: Harvard University Press.

4. Two seminal contributions are Alasdair MacIntyre's *After Virtue. A Study in Moral Theory*. 3rd edition. (London: Duckworth, 2000 [1981]) and Michael J. Sandel, *Justice: What's the Right Thing to Do?* (London: Penguin, 2009).

5. Jo Cox's maiden speech in the House of Commons, Wednesday 3 June 2015. Transcript available at https://www.parliament.uk/business/news/2016/june/jo-cox-maiden-speech-in-the-house-of-commons

6. See Milbank, J. and Pabst, A. (2016) *The Politics of Virtue: Post-liberalism and the Human Future*. London: Rowman & Littlefield International, pp.69–90.

7. Pabst, A. (2017) 'Post-liberalism: The New Centre-ground of British Politics.' *The Political Quarterly*, 88, 3.

8. See again Milbank, J. and Pabst, A. (2016) *The Politics of Virtue: Post-liberalism and the Human Future*. London: Rowman, pp.69–90.

9. Goodhart, D. (2017) T*he Road to Somewhere: The Populist Revolt and the Future of Politics*. London: Hurst.

10. Pope Paul VI. (1965) *Gaudium et spes*. Vatican City: The Vatican, 7.

11. Pontifical Council for Justice and Peace. (2004) Compendium of the Social Doctrine of the Church. Vatican City: The Vatican, 164, 2.

12. Relational goods involve three properties: reciprocity (give-and-take), gratuitousness (the sole purpose of a relational good is the relationship, not some return) and the good (relational goods are not commodities that have a market price).

13. Bruni, L. and Zamagni, S. (2016) *Civil Economy: Another Idea of the Market*. Newcastle: Agenda Publishing Ltd, pp.101–112.

14. See (among other works) Taylor, C. (2003) *Modern Social Imaginaries*. Durham, NC: Duke University Press.

15. Pope Francis. (2016) 'Message for the World Day of Migrants and Refugees 2016.' The Vatican, 17 January, 2016.

2

Migration, Morality and States

Ben Ryan

Few debates have become as polarising, or seemingly intractable, in British public life as the future of immigration policy. At the heart of the failure to deliver any consensus is an absence of any shared values structure that would define a British approach to dealing with the question of migration.

This failing is not unique to the UK; in fact, it has come to be a broader hole at the heart of the West. From Hungary, Poland and Greece to the USA and Canada, and from Finland and Norway to Australia and New Zealand, the West is struggling to reconcile itself to (at least potentially) irreconcilable principles on migration. Policies strain simultaneously to be maximally economically beneficial and simultaneously maximally able to protect social cohesion and avoid the undermining of national identity. The common feature across these policies is that they have all come to put the needs of the state as the primary criteria by which to assess migration.

In trying to form a migration policy with a moral basis to it this is a critical issue. If migration is to be assessed only according to the needs of the state (whether economic or socio-political) what, if anything, is the moral basis to that policy? Can states act morally, or will their self-interest inevitably come at the expense of individual migrants? This chapter argues that without a moral core that extends far beyond the interest of the state to focus migration policy it will always be in crisis – oscillating between competing state interests without being firmly grounded in any overriding principle.

To that end, this chapter will begin by considering the unexpected revival of the nation state (particularly the UK in the context of the 2016 Brexit vote), and how migration can pose both problems and advantages for this political unit. It will then look at the means by which states can respond to those advantages and disadvantages to further their own interests, and the impact this has upon migrants. It will conclude with a call for a new, moral settlement to migration policy which puts the human person and a rights-based model as the long-term basis for future policy.

The unexpected revival of the nation state

For much of modern European history the basic unit of international politics has been the nation state. The nation, for which the European model was taken from the biblical accounts of Israel as a single people sharing some common identifying aspects such as a shared language, ethnicity, history and religion (the latter, in a Europe with declining religious affiliation) is often overlooked today, but was critical in earlier formulations. The state, by contrast, is a construction which is, theoretically, purely political and regardless of the identity of people – it is simply a bordered space within which everything and everyone is under a single government.

The creation of the nation state bound these two concepts together – a single homogeneous, bounded community. The theory of international relations for much of the twentieth century was that this was the best possible model for assuring peaceful and harmonious international politics. Theoretically such units are maximally stable, being less prone to internal division than other political entities, with a united people under a single government.

In fact, this was always less evident in practice than in theory – for precious few of the world's states are true nation states. The UK is a prime example, consisting of at least four indigenous nations (English, Welsh, Scottish and Irish – with debates to be had over the status of groups such as the Cornish). Nevertheless, this model has been promoted consistently for much of at least the twentieth century as the political ideal – with the consequences clearly visible in, for example, British foreign policy in dividing up India and Pakistan so as to create new nation states, or in the continued promotion of the 'two state solution' as the most durable future for peace in the Middle East.

There was a period, however, in the last decades of the twentieth and even in the first few years of the twenty-first centuries when it looked as though the nation state was a species on the verge of extinction. The European project, begun in the 1950s was growing and looked to be the future. In 1994 the newly constituted European Union looked like the future. By 2004, when it had expanded to 25 states, with a commitment to removing internal borders the progress away from the nation state model seemed inevitable.[1]

What we are seeing today is a radical return to prominence for the nation state, and a corresponding collapse in the appeal of supranational solutions. Brexit is one symptom of this wider trend – a rejection of past confidence in international unions and projects in favour of a return to a more robust, nation state-centred politics (other symptoms include the rise of Donald Trump, and a slew of populist nationalist leaders across Europe, including Russia's Vladimir Putin, Hungary's Viktor Orbán and Poland's Andrzej Duda). The Leave campaigners are typical of this wider trend of calling for a return of sovereignty and control, and the ability to protect the nation from outsiders and foreign interference.

This revival of the demands for a robust nation state goes hand in hand with a rejection of supra-nationalism. The early European project hoped to control the nation state, using economic ties to build a 'solidarity'.[2] The dream of the 1950s, driven through by a committed cadre of predominately Catholic European leaders, was to limit the likelihood of war and economic competition that would damage living and working conditions by proposing a new international politics.[3] That vision has long been under strain, and Brexit may prove to be the beginning of the end for supranational political bodies. At the same time, it is not only political supranationalism that is coming under strain. Economic globalisation is losing its lustre too, with increasing calls for returns to protectionist economic policies and resistance to global multinationals.

At the centre of the political debate is the spectre of immigration and control of the border. Migration poses a particular challenge to the nation state, and as a result has become arguably the single most critical political (and ethical) issue of our time. Quite why migration poses such a problem for the nation state is the issue to which this essay now turns.

Migration as a challenge to the nation state

The idea that the nation state provides the most durable political unit, and best guarantor of peace, remains much in vogue. It has a strong basis in international law. For example, the concept of self-determination holds that 'all peoples have the right to self-determination, by virtue of economic, social and cultural development'.[4] This is not uncontested, not least since what constitutes a 'people' has never been adequately defined.

The underlying assumption, both in this international legal sense, and more broadly among advocates for a nation state model is that a people are a recognisably homogeneous grouping, bound by such markers as race, language, shared cultural features and religion. The resulting logic of this is that if that internal homogeneity is undermined, then the nation state itself becomes vulnerable.

It is this fear that underpins a great political energy. The Brexit referendum was fought on a number of issues, but immigration was clearly critical. It is also a feature of a growing library of books and articles that warn of a British nation state being fatally undermined. The right-wing commentator Douglas Murray, for example, devotes a large part of his book to the idea that immigration, and the political acceptance of immigration as normal, is killing European and British culture.[5] He laments in particular that in London, the 'white British' are now a minority in 'their' own capital.

If the nation state rests on a homogeneous national identity, then there is some reason for concern when it comes to migration. One is a basic numbers game – a fear that too many outsiders will come to literally outnumber those who are insiders, without ever becoming insiders themselves. Thus predictions that Muslims will outnumber the rest of the population by 2066,[6] or notes about so-called 'white flight' (when white British people leave an area that is becoming perceived as an immigrant area) reflect that fear of being outnumbered and replaced.

However, there is also a broader cultural sense in which migration seems to threaten the nation state, which is whether newly arrived cultures, rather than people, start to replace the existing culture. This might be in a relatively active sense, with foreign traditions and culture being added into the mix (contemporary British cuisine, for example, is clearly marked by influences from abroad, particularly Indian sub-continental traditions). That aspect tends to be less controversial. More difficult is the accusation that British culture is called to mute itself in order to integrate others.

This latter sense is what drives much of the controversy over 'political correctness'. While it may never have been true that a council banned the word 'Christmas' or tried to replace it with 'Winterval', the reason these stories tend to take off is the truth that people fear that it has become somehow inappropriate to assert a British identity for fear of causing offence. This sense of a culture killing itself by amnesia, or deliberate downplaying of its own distinctiveness is a real fear and not without basis. As shall be returned to below in the section on assimilation, this is a critical fault line in debates over immigration. How far is an immigrant expected to become British? Indeed, even beyond that, is it possible for someone to simply become British at all?

Twenty-seven years ago, Norman Tebbit first introduced his 'cricket test', asking immigrants which country they would support in a cricket match between England and India or Pakistan. And, today, the UK has still not formed a clear expectation of what ideal immigrant integration should look like. In fact, in the wake of increased fears over international terrorism, particularly among Muslims, these questions seem to be becoming more urgent, but without any greater clarity over the answers. As an entity that relies on a perceived homogeneity, the nation state is under threat from levels of migration that, worldwide, are unquestionably higher than they have ever been.[7]

Of course, that does not tell the whole story, and migration has also been encouraged or supported at a policy level for the assets it brings to the state.

Migration as an asset to the state
The immediate beneficiaries of migration policy are, generally speaking, migrants themselves. The other key beneficiary has been the state itself. Herein we see an example of the muddle of values governing migration policy. Migration is both a threat to the model of the nation state, and yet in another sense the nation state is a beneficiary of migration.

The most important gain for the state is in the provision of labour. The need for workers in key areas has underpinned a number of immigration policies, including the Australian Skilled Immigrants Points Test, which was also proposed by leading Brexiteers Michael Gove and Boris Johnson as a possible model for a post-Brexit UK immigration policy. The UK, in fact, already has a points system of sorts, introduced under Labour in 2008 which applies to non-EU migrants (EU migrants at the time of writing enjoy free movement under EU law, subject to likely changes in the future). This assigns migrants to four possible tiers (high value, skilled worker, student, temporary migrant) each of which requires points in order to be afforded a visa. The easiest means to achieve a high number of points is to be on the 'Shortage Occupation List' which includes jobs deemed most needed in the British economy.

The intention of the Gove and Johnson strategy was to build on that and extend the model across all migration policy. Quite what rights and status these economic migrants would have is a matter of debate. At the extreme end, several Middle Eastern states operate a system of 'guest workers' from abroad, who are afforded no or very few working rights and, in the case of several countries (including Qatar), can never apply for permanent residency or citizenship under any circumstances. This (as explored further below) would present a number of challenges in terms of how to guard against the exploitation of such workers, and how to promote integration.

Aside from economic benefits there is also an aspect which is more closely tied to the cultural question of identity. A fascinating example of this was the debate, spearheaded by the actress Joanna Lumley, around the Gurkha Justice Campaign. The debate was over the rights to immigrate to Britain for Gurkha veterans who had served in the British army. The campaign received widespread support from some surprising sources, notably the generally anti-migrant Daily Mail. In this case migration became something that was not about undermining the nation state, but about affirming a British vision of service, patriotism and fairness.

Other examples, though not as marked as the Gurkha case (in that there is less widespread support in these cases), can be seen in support for immigration from the Commonwealth, which affirms cultural, historic and linguistic ties, and support for refugees, affirming a tradition of responsibility and compassion.

These cases are significantly less likely than economic factors to be widely accepted as benefits of migration for the state. As a cultural issue it falls some way short of the challenges to the nation state model noted above. The economic gains, by contrast, have been used as a means of supporting immigration within the nation state model, particularly when it comes to the establishment of the 'market state' (see below).

Techniques and strategies: how the nation state has responded to the challenge of migration

In response to the challenges outlined above nation states have adopted a number of tactics to maximise their own interests. The most common four have been multiculturalism, the adoption of the market state, assimilation and securitisation. Each of these four tactics poses some fairly major ethical and moral challenges.

1. Multiculturalism

Multiculturalism, here understood as a political ideology rather than simply as a normative description, has long had its critics. It was adopted by the Canadian government of Pierre Trudeau in the 1970s and 1980s and the UK government of Tony Blair in the late 1990s and early 2000s. It is often characterised as a policy designed to let all cultures and faiths live alongside one another without any efforts at assimilation, though that is to over-generalise what was proposed in both Canada and the UK.[8]

Fair or unfair, the accusation that this policy failed to meaningfully build national loyalty or solidarity among minority and migrant groups has led to it largely being abandoned. What was hoped to be a policy that would build cohesive society instead has become perceived as creating a ghettoisation of communities that was never going to be conducive to the promotion of the common good or meaningful integration. At its worst, it falls into a classic liberal trap, which is to mistake tolerance for love. This was a point made by the Catholic priest Tomáš Halík in a 2014 lecture. Halík noted that Jesus' astonishing command to love your neighbour demanded more than accepting them and leaving them to their own devices. Meaningful community requires more than acceptance, it demands some genuine encounter.[9]

A failure to encourage any meaningful form of encounter raises the prospect of migrants never becoming a full part of the British nation, or even contributing towards it, and of a nation state undermined as communities suffer for a lack of cohesion. As a result, this strategy has been largely abandoned and carries reservations as to how effective it can ever be at forming an adequate response to the issue of migration.

2. The market state

A second tactic adopted by states has been to, in effect, side-line the issue of internal homogeneity by instead recasting the nation state as the market state. In this scenario, cultural and societal markers are downplayed in favour of a purely economic assessment of human worth. This has been particularly used as the tactic for dealing with migrants, who are accepted or rejected based purely on their ability to contribute to the national economy.

This is commonly seen in migration policies that admit migrants primarily on the basis of labour market needs. It is worth noting on this point that Western nations have tended (despite recent trends) to be relatively generous in admitting migrants and allowing them to apply for citizenship.

This compares very favourably to other parts of the world. For example, Middle Eastern states have historically encouraged a high degree of labour movement, but minimal levels of citizenship. In fact, by comparison to Western Europe, the Middle East has seen significantly higher labour migration. By the early 1980s foreign workers made up 70 per cent of Kuwait's workforce, 81 per cent of Qatar's, 40 per cent of Bahrain's, 85 per cent of the UAE's and 75 per cent of Saudi Arabia's.[10] Jordan was forced in that period to import foreign workers in order to replace those Jordanians who had gone to work in its oil-producing neighbours. These states wanted foreign labour, but certainly did not want to expand their citizenship to cover this vast number of foreigners, or even to support many labour and social rights. This is a perfect example of a 'market state' mentality that embraces migrants as part of a work-force, and yet has no interest in assimilating them into the state.

The problem is that this system causes a number of abuses. Since these workers are not citizens their rights and status are not protected by the state in which they work, but their own state.

The ability of their own state to lobby for and protect the rights of workers is limited. In the case of the several million foreign workers in Saudi Arabia, there has been a tendency for states to be more concerned with maintaining good diplomatic relationships and the ability to continue to export labour (in the case of some, like the Philippines, a key asset to their own economy) than to protect workers overseas.

No one is proposing that the UK adopt the indentured labour model of the Middle East. However, the question about who supports the rights of migrants who are seen as little more than grist for the national economic mill is a serious one. At present the UK is bound by European law, which provides an international standard for the rights of workers within the UK. The intention of the current government (at the time of writing) to withdraw from the European Court of Justice (ECJ) would remove that check and balance, and it is not yet clear what protections for migrant workers will pass into British law.

There are several other reasons to resist this approach to migration and citizenship. One is that such a policy has been shown time and again to cause resentment, as native workers feel undermined and that their wages have been depressed due to undercutting. This is both bad for social cohesion and makes such workers a target for potential abuse. It is also the potential flaw in any policy that proposes temporary working visas for migrant workers. Such a system may reduce the number of dependants migrants bring into a country (and correspondingly lower any strain on public services), but it does not answer the criticism that these workers undercut British workers. In fact, it runs the risk of exacerbating current tensions, since without families attending British schools and other public activities and services there is even less reason for migrants to attempt to integrate, learn the language or work to help build cohesive communities.

Furthermore, this policy risks de-humanising migrants. People are turned into nothing more than commodified labour, valued only in so far as they contribute to the economic machine. This is reflected throughout in migrant policies that are defined purely in terms of interests. The interests of the state, employers and the labour market come to dominate discourse on migrant policy. Notable in this is that migration policies rarely, if ever, seem to reflect the interests of individual migrants. This perpetuates a dehumanised vision of migrants, or in the words of Pope Francis:

> *The prevailing mentality puts the flow of people at the service of the flow of capital, resulting in many cases in the exploitation of employees as if they were objects to be used, discarded and thrown out.*[11]

There is also a sense in which this prioritises a very particular conception of labour, namely what eighteenth-century economists like Adam Smith would have termed 'productive labour'. Productive labour is that which contributes to the wealth of society at large. The question is whether wealth is the same thing as value to society.

Caring, whether that is for the sick, the elderly, children and family members, provides some economic value, but its true value lies in its social and moral value. It is important work that contributes towards the common good but which has little economic value. Without these sorts of labour it would be impossible to have a functioning society.

Similarly, volunteering, or work within the charity sector, is unlikely to meet most criteria of 'productive labour' or be able to demonstrate that it creates a significant degree of wealth. However, this work also is critical to a functioning society. In the UK austerity cuts to public services have left the voluntary sector providing an increasingly significant range of services, from childcare to mental health provision, and from foodbanks to employment training. This work is essential, and though it is sometimes calculated as a whole to provide significant economic gains (the NCVO estimate that the voluntary sector is worth £12.2bn)[12] it is rarely valued as such when assessing the value of individuals.

The market state model, therefore, raises the dangers of abusing migrant workers, of stoking resentment and of dehumanising migrants into productive labour units, which fail to recognise the full breadth of valuable labour. As a model it falls someway short of an optimal solution.

3. Assimilation

Promoting integration by assimilation is a policy that seems to be growing in popularity across the globe. A glance at the development of citizenship tests in countries like the USA and the UK, for example, shows that such tests are becoming more difficult and demand greater levels of assimilation than ever before. Compulsory language classes for migrants are a policy that has grown over recent years. A Council of Europe report found that, in 2010, 23 states (of the 31 that responded to the survey) made language knowledge a requirement for admission to the country, permanent residence or acquisition of citizenship.[13]

Languages are a soft aspect of assimilation. Harder asks include the demands for oaths of allegiance – despite the fact that the evidence for the success of these in promoting integration is limited[14] – or in particular demands about dress, religious observance and cultural behaviours. In the West such debates have tended to particularly revolve around a perceived problem with Islam. Bans on particular items of clothing, such as the Hijab, are one such example.

Jonathan Fox[15] has identified 30 separate types of religious discrimination used by states. These discriminatory policies tend to be used to enforce the homogeneity of the in-group by undermining minority groups. In Fox's study he looks at the treatment of Muslims in 26 Western democracies, and the treatment of Christians in 17 Middle Eastern Muslim-majority states.

He concludes that policies against Muslims in the West appear to be on the rise, with 16 of the 30 types of religious discrimination present in at least one Western democracy (this book was written in 2008 and the trend is likely to have increased since). He does, nonetheless, note that the discrimination does not tend to be overly systematic. Only three of these restrictions at that time appeared in more than two or three Western states. Things were significantly worse in the surveyed Middle Eastern countries (which reiterates the point that these are not by any means exclusively, or even primarily, Western failings). Twenty-eight types of discrimination were tracked against Christians in the Middle East. In 14 countries Christians are barred from proselytising, and in 12 Muslims are banned from converting to Christianity. There are 11 states in which Christian pupils in public schools have to take classes in Islam, and six in which Muslims are given preference over Christians in custody cases.

We can conclude from this that policies based heavily around assimilation have the potential to seriously hurt minority groups, and in any context carry the possibility of despotic tendencies and serious discrimination. In attempting to ensure the homogeneity of the community, the temptation is either to exclude migrants and minorities, or else force their assimilation at the expense of their own beliefs and practices.

There is clearly a balance to be struck here. The majority of British citizens would like to see migrants learn English[16] and to be integrated into British society. The question is about the extent to which assimilation implies the elimination of other identities, and how far that should be enforced, rather than merely encouraged.

4. Securitisation

In common with several of the above responses securitisation is a policy (or set of policies) that reflects a treatment of migrants entirely from the perspective of state interest. In this case, migrants are assessed in terms of the risk they pose as a direct security threat, rather than the more cultural threat of undermining homogeneity that underpins the assimilation tactic. In many Western states this agenda has come to define migration policy, particularly in relation to accepting refugees.

The executive order signed by President Trump soon after entering office that bans refugees and migrants from states including Syria, Yemen and Iran among others is a prominent and extreme version of this agenda, but is not unique. Policies in Poland, Hungary and elsewhere also prioritise security as a prime agenda, though in Eastern Europe this is often combined with the cultural aspect – with refugees taken only from Christian backgrounds. These are deemed to be safer, and more in keeping in with the culture of their new home.

While recognising that states do have a duty to protect their own citizens it is clear that, much like the market state approach, this agenda falls into the trap of de-humanising and de-personalising migrants. There is no good reason to assume that all people from these countries pose a blanket risk to the safety of American citizens. In addition a securitising agenda leads to understandable feelings of resentment among migrant groups, and can impact upon their ability to feel integrated into society. This in turn may, itself, prove a barrier to integration and a longer-term security risk.

A note on refugees

This chapter has been concerned with migration as a whole. It has not, so far, particularly paid attention to the refugee issue. This is partly because, despite the prevalence of refugees in media discourses about migration, they make up only a small part of the picture. The ONS figures for 2016 reveal that there were 38,517 asylum applications. This is certainly a large number, but in a context of a total immigration of 596,000 it makes up just 6.5 per cent of migrants.

However, refugees reveal part of the broader issue at the heart of all the models discussed above. As with migration more broadly, the debate is centred around the interests of states and the security agenda. Refugee policy across the West has been more and more centred on the issues of what states can afford to do, and what risks are entailed in taking on refugees. Notable in this is the trend of de-humanising or de-personalising refugees, and a downgrading of ideas of justice and the needs of vulnerable individuals in favour of a state-interest led model.

The trend of de-humanising the issue is also apparent in the way in which the system as a whole seems purpose built to deter human agency and dignity. A narrative has been created that divides refugees into 'good' and 'bad' sets.[17] 'Good' refugees are those that stay in camps and wait to be processed. They are the passive recipients of care from other states and ought to wait until they have been deemed sufficiently acceptable to a state's interest to be permitted access. By contrast 'bad' refugees are those that do not wait in the conditions of the camps but attempt to help themselves through their own agency by attempting to travel to a new country of their own choosing, perhaps by attempting to cross the Mediterranean. These 'bad' refugees are deemed to be jumping the queue, and are particularly likely to be subject to fears stemming from the securitisation agenda. In a sense this reiterates the extent to which debates over migration have become excessively focused on the interests of states and the de-humanising of migrants, whether refugees or not.

Breaking the state model: towards a new moral underpinning for migration policy

So far this chapter has argued that at the heart of debates about migration is the issue of the nation state itself. This political unit has, in some ways surprisingly, survived and even flourished in recent years. With that has come consequences. Migration poses a challenge to the bounded homogeneity of the nation state, yet has become an economic necessity, and the resulting strategies to control migration each come with significant problems. The multiculturalism model provides little basis for the forming of true solidarity in society. The market state model dehumanises migrants and makes them into nothing more than commodified labour, with little hope of meaningful cohesion. Assimilation runs the risk of becoming oppressive, and at any rate seems a poor match with the economic priority. Securitisation again dehumanises migrants.

In each case, critically, the focus has primarily been placed on how migration affects the interests of nation states, rather than the needs, wishes or agency of migrants themselves. Global levels of migration have reached unprecedented levels over recent years, which combined with the recovery of the nation state makes a need for a new settlement one of increasing urgency. Too great a focus on the nation state without a cohesive values structure will see the chaotic approach to migration continue – with the UK oscillating between obsessions with national cohesion and identity, on the one hand, and economic gains on the other.

1. A humanised model

The first and critical principle for a new Christian model is that any and all approaches to the question of citizenship or migration policy must start from the simple position that those involved are human beings imbued with human dignity. This simple message is critical to any genuinely Christian model of politics or society and is far too often overlooked in current policy.

Christian anthropology rests on the principle that all humans are made in the image of God. Furthermore, the equal dignity of humanity is established in a salvation which is not limited by any racial, gender or social status. The special status of humanity, made in the image of God, demands that we treat one another in the same light – as equally imbued with an essential dignity and a special status in the eyes of God.

As such the reduction of human beings to nothing more than economic units, or commodities, is an affront to the idea of human dignity. In place of the recognition of humanity the approaches of the market state, in particular, tend towards an idolatrous obsession with economic progress at the expense of human dignity. Pope Francis's Encyclical powerfully argues that:

The worship of the ancient golden calf (cf. Ex 32:1–35) has returned in a new and ruthless guise in the idolatry of money and the dictatorship of an impersonal economy lacking a truly human purpose. The worldwide crisis affecting finance and the economy lays bare their imbalances and, above all, their lack of real concern for human beings; man is reduced to one of his needs alone: consumption.[19]

The point about recognising human dignity naturally takes on a particular importance in the case of refugees. As argued above the system of many states currently seems to actively deny any dignity or agency to refugees themselves, leaving them as nothing more than a security threat or economic assessment to be made by states.

2. The balance between rights and responsibilities
Having established the need for a model of citizenship and the treatment of migrants which prioritises human dignity, there is a need to establish what that might look like in practice. Most debates around citizenship ultimately come down to a clash between a communitarian approach which stresses the need for responsibilities on citizens,[20] and an individualist approach that stresses a rights model.[21]

The advantage of a rights model is that it recognises the dignity of each human being and defines their rights as an individual. There are, of course, a number of international human rights treaties which affect the status of individuals and which might serve as models for an extension of the system. For example, the UN Convention Relating to the Status of Refugees guarantees the rights of anyone claiming asylum, preventing them from being expelled (Article 32) or forcibly returned (Article 33) and guaranteeing, among other things, their freedom of religion (Article 4).

Similarly, in the case of migrant workers, a possible model lies in the International Convention on the Protection of the Rights of All Migrant Workers and Members of their Families. Its scope is limited, not least because it has only 38 signatories.

There is a model in international law, therefore, for an extension of the human rights model. There is also a strong Christian basis for a more rights-based approach. On the topic of migrants in particular the Old Testament has a fairly developed set of rights which it attaches to the *gerim* (sojourners, settled foreigners). Among other things there is a clear prohibition against abuse of foreigners (Leviticus 19.33–34), a call for equal treatment of foreigners before the law (Leviticus 24.22; Deuteronomy 1.16) and the call for those who have integrated into the community to be included in the feasts and festivals of Israel (Exodus 12.48; Deuteronomy 31.12).

There are dangers in overemphasising the importance of rights. Human beings are body, mind and soul, and their political and civic identity reflects that in so far as a rights-based model of citizenship appeals most to the mind – it is the logical, and legal sense of being protected and guaranteed a particular status. A more communitarian model might view citizenship more as a matter of the soul – of real essential belonging to a place and, therefore, what a citizen owes to the state. This mind against soul battle for the authentic nature of citizenship has always characterised the debate.[22]

Just as rights have a strong Christian pedigree in talking about citizenship, so too the more communitarian approach can claim a Christian heritage. In a 2001 essay, Archbishop Vincent Nichols argued that '"Solidarity" is the Christian word for citizenship.'[23] In seeking a balance, however, too many states at present have over-emphasised the responsibilities required of migrants and minorities in particular, with the interest of the state having come to excessively outweigh the dignity of individual people.

3. The common good beyond state borders
The difficulty in rebalancing the scales between individual rights and collective responsibility lies in the continuing role of states

as the ultimate arbiters of citizenship. If rights are only defined according to the state then there is a clear potential contest between the state's own interests (in terms of the securitisation or market needs discussed above) and the interests of individuals seeking citizenship and their families. The only effective means to guarantee a more Christian conception of citizenship that prioritises human dignity over state economic pressures is with a more extensive and robust international legal framework.

This can be overstated. There is no need to move all the way to a fully cosmopolitan system that precludes all sense of national borders. The Old Testament demands for the legal rights of sojourners never amount to total equality with Israelites. Sojourners could not, for example, become king (Deuteronomy 17.15). Nor does a rights-based approach entirely solve the issue of state interests – since in practice, acting to protect these rights will still require states as agents.

However, it is to argue that an ethical model for the UK's future migration policy needs to be part of an extended model of international law that guarantees a minimum level of rights. Critically, this needs to be underpinned by an international system that will guard against the dominance of state interests over individuals. Breaking the model of the nation state as the locus of all political and civic identity is essential in this. As long as citizenship is envisaged only as a filing system for dividing people according to state authority,[24] the problems outlined above will continue.

The responsibilities of migrants can (and must) still be emphasised and encouraged. States ought certainly to be mindful of protecting themselves from dangerous elements. Those resident ought to work to contribute towards the common good (to 'seek the welfare of the city' in the words of Jeremiah 29.7) and to attempt to integrate into wider society. A rights-based model in fact can aid that process of integration. With a fuller set of rights to participate in all aspects of society, whether as a migrant worker or as a minority group within a country, more opportunities for integration can emerge. Instead of creating a stratified society with an underclass who lack the ability to work in some areas, manifest their beliefs or participate in civic and political life, a freer society can provide opportunities for more rapid and lasting integration.[25]

A model of migration and status underpinned by an international human rights model has much to recommend it in Christian terms, not least in nuancing the idea of neighbourliness beyond state and ethnic boundaries. The question 'who is my neighbour' (Luke 10.29) is a critical question here. Jesus' answer is to provide the parable of the Good Samaritan. However else that parable is to be understood, one point that seems incontestable is that neighbourliness goes beyond the bounded community. Samaritans and Jews are different peoples, yet the responsibility of care transcends that difference.

This then is the core of how a new approach to immigration might work. One that humanises migrants, rather than reducing them to commodities or de-personalised threats. One that commits to the idea of contribution to the common good and the need for migrants to work to that end, but which redresses the balance between rights and responsibilities by committing to an international rights model that breaks migration away from a matter that is simply assessed according to the interests of the nation state. Such a model would take bold political leadership, particularly in the current political climate, but would establish a migration policy that was clear in its own values structure and moral foundations.

ENDNOTES

1. Milward, A. (2016) *The European Rescue of the Nation-State*. Oxford: Routledge.
2. The Schuman Declaration, May 9, 1950.
3. Ryan, B. (2017) *A Soul for the Union*. London: Theos.
4. United National Declaration on the Granting of Independence to Colonial Countries and Peoples. Article 2. General Assembly Resolution 1514, XV, 14 December, 1960.

5. Murray, D. (2017) *The Strange Death of Europe*. London: Bloomsbury.

6. Brown, M. (2013) 'Migrants change UK forever: White Britons "will be in minority by 2066".' *Daily Express*, 2 May, 2013.

7. The UN report of 2015 ('International Migration Report 2015', UN 2016) put the total number of migrants worldwide at 244 million, up from the previous high of 222 million in 2010.

8. For a more in-depth discussion of multiculturalism, see Mohammed Girma's chapter below.

9. Halík was speaking in London at a ceremony to mark his winning of the Templeton Prize, May 14, 2014.

10. Humphrey, M. (1993) 'Migrants, Workers and Refugees: The Political Economy of Population Movements in the Middle East.' *Middle East Report 181*, Radical Movements: Migrants, Workers and Refugees.

11. From an address given by Pope Francis, 17 February 17 2016 'Meeting with the world of labour.'

12. National Council for Voluntary Organizations. (2017) 'British Social Attitudes: Record number of Brits with no religion.' UK Civil Society Almanac 2017. London: National Centre for Social Research.

13. Extramiana, C. and Van Avermaet, P. (2011) 'Language requirements for adult migrants in Council of Europe member states: Report on a survey'. Strasbourg: Council of Europe, Language Policy Division.

14. See El-Haj, T.R.A. (2009) 'Becoming Citizens in an Era of Globalization and Transnational Migration: Re-Imagining Citizenship as Critical Practice'. *Theory into Practice*, 48, 4, 274–282 and Maxwell, R. (2010) 'Evaluating Migrant Integration: Political Attitudes Across Generations in Europe.' *The International Migration Review*. 44, 1.

15. Fox, J. (2008) *A World Survey of Religion and the State*. Cambridge: Cambridge University Press.

16. They also want the government to play a role in this – a recent report (Sunder Katwala, Jill Rutter and Steve Ballinger, *Time to get it right: Finding consensus on Britain's future immigration policy* (London: British Future, 2017)) found that 67 per cent of the British public think the government should be providing more language classes.

17. This is an idea explored at some length by Mavelli, L. and Wilson, E.K. (2017) *The Refugee Crisis and Religion: Secularism, Security and Hospitality in Question*. London: Rowman and Littlefield.

18. Maxwell, R. (2010) 'Evaluating Migrant Integration: Political Attitudes Across Generations in Europe.' *The International Migration Review*. 44, 1.

19. Pope Francis. (2013). *Evangelii gaudium*. Vatican City: The Vatican.

20. E.g. Shafiq, M. (1998) 'Immigration Theology in Islam.' In Timani, H., Jorgenson, A. and Hwang, A. (2015) *Strangers in this World: Multireligious Reflections on Immigration.* Minneapolis: Fortress.

21. E.g. Rawls, J. (1972) *A Theory of Justice.* Oxford: Oxford University Press.

22. See for example Stapleton, J. (2005) 'Citizenship versus Patriotism in Twentieth-Century England.' *The Historical Journal*, 48, 1, 151–178.

23. Nichols, V. (2001) 'The Common Good.' In Alton, D. (2001) *Citizen 21: Citizenship in the New Millennium.* London: HarperCollins Publishers Ltd.

24. As described by Brubaker, R. (1992) *Citizenship and Nationhood in France and Germany.* Cambridge MA: Harvard University Press.

25. Maxwell, R. (2010) 'Evaluating Migrant Integration: Political Attitudes Across Generations in Europe.' *The International Migration Review*, 44, 1.

3

The Future of Migration is Temporary

David Goodhart, Policy Exchange

The most important story about immigration into rich countries (including, but by no means exclusively, the UK) in the next generation will be the growing importance of temporary immigration.

A greater use of temporary immigration, with a clearer distinction between temporary and permanent citizens, is the most plausible way of squaring the circle between responding to the democratic pressure to reduce numbers while still maintaining quite high inflows of relevant migrants into rich countries.

This is particularly important for the UK as it enters the Brexit period with public opinion still strongly in favour of reducing recent levels of immigration and yet an economy that has become unusually dependent on EU-based migrant labour in both skilled and unskilled sectors.

But it should also be the broad direction of travel for almost all rich countries in order to be able combine a degree of economic and cultural openness without inflicting 'brain drain' on poorer countries, permanently stripping them of their best educated and most energetic people.

This stress on temporary immigration is also based on certain assumptions about the objections that people have to mass immigration in Western countries. This is no longer mainly xenophobic, though xenophobes remain. It is about fears, often legitimate, of economic competition and also, even more important, about over-rapid cultural change. People generally prefer the familiar to the strange, and living in stable communities with some degree of neighbourliness to living in low-trust transit zones.

A clear majority of British people believe that high immigration undermines rather than enriches the national culture. And opposition to immigration is significantly higher in those wards that are experiencing the most rapid ethnic change.[1] There is plenty of evidence from both common sense and observation that suggests it is easier to absorb numbers of people into already existing communities with relatively strong common norms.

Lower levels of permanent immigration slow the pace of ethnic-demographic change which is one of the main, albeit seldom articulated, sources of resistance to mass migration. It thereby also lowers public anxiety about integration of minorities and the sharing of public goods with newcomers.

There are, of course, various objections to moving in this direction but none, I think, are decisive. They can be grouped together under three main headings: enforcement, human rights and integration.

On enforcement, how is it possible prevent temporary migrants becoming permanent ones without an intrusive and expensive bureaucracy to enforce their temporary status?

On human rights, the whole thrust of human rights legislation in recent years has been to reduce the distinction between citizens and non-citizens living within the same political-legal space and human rights law generally sets its face against two-tier citizenship, seeing it as discriminatory.

And on integration, if people are here for only a short period they will have little incentive to learn the language or become part of British social networks and, critics suggest, this will exacerbate the integration problem. I will address these reservations later in this essay.

Where are we now?

First of all, it is important to consider the nature of current inflows and understand just how significant temporary migration is. In recent years the gross annual immigration inflow to the UK – meaning people coming to live in the UK for one year or more – has been between 500,000 and 600,000 a year, with a net figure ranging between 250,000 and 350,000 a year.[2] The largest flows are work related, followed by students, family reunion and refugees. All of these flows, with the exception of family reunion, have a substantial temporary element. Taking immigration as a whole, more than half is probably now temporary, meaning people staying for less than five years.

Indeed, the number of immigrants who are granted permanent residence in the UK has fallen quite sharply in recent years. From a high of 241,586 in 2010 it has fallen (partly for technical reasons) to a low of 57,111 in the year ending March 2017.[3] (It will be rising again sharply in the next few years but largely as a result of EU citizens who have lived here for more than five years claiming permanent residence to mitigate the uncertainties of Brexit.)

One of the reasons that the number is so low is because people coming from the EU to work or study, around half of the net immigration inflow, have not in recent years needed permanent residence in order to enjoy the benefits and security of British citizenship.

But the numbers acquiring permanent residence from the EU has also been in decline. Most current non-EU visa routes for study and work are time limited though, in some cases, can be extended to the five years that normally allows people to apply for permanent residence (for students it is nine years).

In the past few years the average number of international (non-EU) students granted an extension on their visa has been about 127,000.[4] There is some dispute about how many out of this number have been staying permanently but research by Migration Watch suggests that in the last seven years about one-quarter have been granted permanent residence. That is more than most people had assumed but it still means that three-quarters are returning home, mainly straight after their three-year-courses.

The most important time limited route from outside the EU for work is the intra-company transfer route (ICT). This is the most important of the so-called Tier 2 routes for skilled workers. There is a general Tier 2 skilled worker route that is not time limited but is capped at 20,700 a year. The ICT is not capped but most workers have to leave after five years (with an extension to nine years in exceptional cases). The number coming through this route for more than one year has increased substantially and, including dependents, amounted to around 60,000 people in 2014. The standard form of ICT is, say, a Japanese employee of Nissan being sent for a two-year period to the UK to help with the launch of a new production line. But in recent years there has been a big increase in so-called third-party contracting in which, for example, an Indian IT consultancy, will send an employee to work for a client of the local branch of the consultancy such as British Airways. About 80 per cent all people coming in under the ICT system are in the IT sector.[5] The ICT system is popular with employers though questions have been raised by the Migration Advisory Committee about whether it can mean reduced training and job opportunities for British workers.[6]

After Brexit the non-permanent ICT route is likely to be used more by EU companies and citizens. And there are two other forms of short-term, non-permanent, immigration schemes that could also play a bigger role after Brexit.

The first is called the Youth Mobility Scheme which has operated successfully for many years. The current scheme allows 18-to-30-year olds to work in the UK for two years with no right of residence. It currently attracts about 50,000 young people a year, with reciprocal quotas in most cases, from Australia, New Zealand, Canada, Japan, Monaco, Hong Kong, South Korea and Taiwan.

Employers in the hospitality sector are particularly keen to extend this scheme to EU countries after Brexit and it might be possible to 'nudge' youth mobility workers towards sectors with shortages.

Another model for short-term, time-limited, migration is the Seasonal Agricultural Workers Scheme (SAWS) which operated relatively successfully for 60 years until it was phased out in 2014 in part because of the large availability of such labour from Eastern Europe. The National Farmers Union (NFU) called it a 'robust and effective' scheme controlled by the UK Border Agency which provided a pool of temporary overseas workers to do outdoor and sometimes physically demanding work in remote locations that is not usually popular with UK workers. The NFU also says that the old SAWS scheme had 'exceptionally high rates of return' at around 98 per cent.[7] Following Brexit the NFU is lobbying to bring back the old SAWS scheme.[8]

Objections: different rights for different stripes

What is being proposed is a kind of humane 'guest worker' scheme for the twenty-first century. As already noted there are several objections. The experience with guest workers from Turkey in several European countries, but above all Germany, in the 1950s and 1960s is often cited in this context and widely regarded as a failure, partly because so many of the guest workers ended up staying but without becoming German citizens. This was considered unfair and bad for integration. But many of the problems with the German story are specific to that time and place.

Turks were not encouraged to take German citizenship, and most did not want to, both because they had come as guest workers but also because neither country recognized dual citizenship and Turks would have lost national rights if they had given up their home citizenship.

So Germany ended up with the worst of all worlds. It had a large group of temporary workers who turned out not be temporary, even after fresh recruitment stopped after 1973. And because they did not take up citizenship the Turks did not have the vote so remained a marginal, introverted group, with even second-generation Turks unable to speak German well, living as a diaspora in their own urban districts. (Compare the invisibility of Turks in German public life, at least until the 1990s, with the much earlier integration of Britain's post-colonial minorities into the political system, especially through the Labour party.)

Today, different kinds of visa status often involve different levels of rights – for example, different kinds of access to the welfare state or the right to bring in dependants. This contrasts with the full rights of a British citizen or someone who has been granted permanent residence. If the government were to move towards a system in which the lion's share of immigration is temporary, there would need to be a clearer differentiation, in the minds of the state, the migrant and the general public, between the rights of the temporary or guest citizen and the full rights of citizenship.

There is likely to be some variation in the rights of temporary citizens – on the right to bring in dependents for example (which is usually allowed for ICT staff) – but the key point is that there should be a clear and binary distinction in the public and official mind between full and temporary citizenship.

The evolution of human rights legislation, including the UK Human Rights Act of 1998, generally opposes such differential rights on grounds of discrimination and wants so far as possible to raise the level of rights for people living within a given jurisdiction whether they are full citizens or not. Experience with asylum cases shows that it can be difficult for governments to deport people once they have lived in a country for a certain number of years, even if they have over-stayed a visa, as they may have acquired ties and connections which, if broken, would amount to an infringement of the right to family life.

So, human rights legislation may make it harder to enforce a clear line between permanent and temporary status, but it will not make it impossible. No rule is uniformly enforceable, and there will, of course, be a number of people who are able, and even encouraged, to jump across the line through marriage, or their value as researchers, artists or skilled employees of various kinds.

But if responsibility for ensuring that temporary visa periods are adhered to is shared with employers, and other public authorities, and countries of origin, there is no reason why many temporaries should end up as permanents. Guest citizenship tied to a three- or four-year work contract would still be very popular for workers at all levels of skill and for people from a range of countries. As we have seen it has worked well in many different forms: seasonal agricultural worker programmes, the youth mobility visa, ICTs and even most students.

And biometric identity cards, initially for all who are not full citizens, and perhaps eventually for all citizens, could help significantly in policing the temporary–permanent line and, indeed, all visa overstaying (by far the largest cause of illegal immigration).

All non-EU immigrants who are here for more than six months, whether as a student or a worker, are already required to hold a biometric ID card. The card contains name, date and place of birth plus biometric information (facial image and fingerprints) and shows an individual's immigration status and social entitlements while they remain in the UK. This allows employers to use the government's free online Biometric Residence Permit checker to establish the right to work.

It also, in principle, allows the NHS, the department of work and pensions, and local authority social services and housing departments to know what the social entitlements of a guest citizen are.

There is often publicly expressed reluctance on the part of health, education and other professionals to act, as they see it, as border guards. But that is usually in the context of illegal immigrants and visa overstayers. Assuming that a clearer divide between temporary and full citizenship is a policy with a high degree of public legitimacy, and has been visibly rolled out by the government, the issue of policing it should not be so fraught.

The principle of a more mutually 'instrumental' relationship between a category of people and British society is not a novel one. Indeed, one might say it already exists for the millions of tourists who visit the country every year. Guest citizens, who one might regard as a special sort of longer-term tourist, would still have the full protection of the law and all the rights and freedoms of our liberal society. They would also have access to the NHS. They would be 'second-class citizens' only in two major respects: their inability to bring in dependents or spouses (and even this might be possible in some cases) and their restricted access to the social state, meaning in and out of work benefits, including tax credits and social housing. (And in return for the reduced access to the social state the guest citizen might pay a special lower rate of income tax.)

The polling evidence suggests that most people are only mild welfare protectionists. They are happy, in other words, to allow people to become part of the national welfare club after just two or three years work and paying into the system. But there is quite strong hostility to people drawing on the full system immediately after they arrive in the country. The idea of 'earned citizenship' is a popular one. But so is the idea of having at least significant part of the welfare state preserved only for full citizens.

Would this work? As Robert Rowthorn has commented (in a pamphlet)[9] it depends on the scale of the 'leakage' which is hard to predict in advance:

> It depends on the willingness of future governments and the courts to formulate and enforce the rules for the temporary worker scheme to operate effectively. The danger is that such a scheme might unravel as governments create ever more exceptions and the courts pick holes in the rules.[10]

Integration and the psychology of temporary citizenship

How would the public in rich countries like Britain respond to a big increase in temporary immigration? Part of the point of devising such a system is premised on the belief that it would reduce anxiety about immigration and allow for larger, albeit temporary, inflows than would be the case with conventional, full citizenship immigration. Critics point out that one of the main sources of anxiety about the current levels of immigration is the difficulty of integrating large numbers of people into British social norms and the British way of life, and that more temporary immigration would simply make this problem worse.

It is true that temporary immigrants would have a reduced incentive to learn English and develop lasting friendships if they were only allowed to stay for a couple of years. On the other hand, the public is likely to have lower expectations of integration of someone who is a guest or temporary citizen. If one of the main causes of immigration-related fear and anxiety is the over-rapid change to the overall demographic order and a sense of social fragmentation then the lack of permanence of migration flows should be a reassuring factor.

People do not, on the whole, worry about the lack of integration of Chinese students who they know, in most cases, are here to study for a few years and are then returning home. But low levels of integration and an economic-instrumental attitude to Britain from, say, Somalis who have permanent residence or Bulgarian or Romanian workers who have to be treated like full citizens (under EU non-discrimination rules, at least prior to Brexit) is a cause of greater discomfort.

If most immigration becomes temporary, it allows, in theory, the welfare state and indeed the very idea of citizenship to be 'ring-fenced' and preserved for insiders, while guest citizens are welcome but unthreatening contributors to the country's economic or cultural vitality. This system would also allow for a clearer concentration of integration efforts, and resources, on newcomers who are staying permanently. With a smaller number of permanent citizens arriving each year – for example, successful asylum seekers and those coming here as spouses and through family reunion programmes – it should be possible to have a better resourced integration programme including free English lessons.

The new mainstream?

Temporary migration with reduced rights for guest citizens is the wave of the future. It has the potential to deal with the democratic rejection of large-scale immigration in rich countries while, at the same time, allowing for continuing mutually beneficial flows of people.

It is widely assumed that future trade deals between blocs or individual countries, especially between developed and developing countries like India, will include labour mobility clauses. But most of these will be temporary arrangements, just another version of today's ICT arrangements which seldom allow for permanent residence.

This idea has certainly become intellectually respectable. Academics such as Martin Ruhs[11] and Branko Milanovic[12] have written about the trade-off between citizen rights and economic immigration. And Dani Rodrik has proposed a global temporary work scheme which would expand the workforce in rich countries by about 3 per cent at any given time (in the UK that would mean about one million workers).[13] Under his scheme a mix of skilled and unskilled workers from poor countries would be allowed to fill jobs in rich countries for a maximum of five years. To ensure that workers return home the programmes would be supported by a range of carrots and sticks applied by both home and host countries. Rodrik estimates that if all rich countries were to implement such a scheme it would boost the global economy by \$360 bn a year.

I have not dwelt here on the broader implications of reducing 'brain drain', but this could be temporary immigration's most important long-term contribution to a more stable and just world. There is plenty of evidence (some of it found in Paul Collier's book *Exodus*[14]) of the damage inflicted, especially on the poorest countries, from losing their brightest and best to rich countries.

As cheaper travel and the internet have created something like a single global society the magnetic attraction of rich Western countries has grown even stronger. Accepting, and even encouraging, the flows may seem virtuous, but it can cause long-term invisible damage and help to unbalance global development.

On the other hand, temporary migration to the West as a student or worker, and ongoing contacts between individuals and institutions in the rich and poor worlds, can help to foster a developmental virtuous circle.

If temporary migration is to become the norm for immigration into rich countries it might require changes to some international agreements and to human rights legislation, both of which might be hard to achieve. But this is surely a prize worth some political struggle to achieve.

ENDNOTES

1. See, for example, Kaufmann, E. and Harris, G. (2014) *Changing Places: Mapping the White Response to Ethnic Change*. London: Demos.

2. Office for National Statistics. (2017) 'Migration statistics quarterly report:' Statistical Bulletin.

3. Office for National Statistics. (2017) 'How many people continue their stay in the UK?' 25 May, 2017.

4. Office for National Statistics. (2016) 'International student migration: What do the statistics tell us?' Population Briefing. January, 2016.

5. Estimated privately by experts in the field.

6. Migration Advisory Committee, December 2015, Review of Tier 2 (Executive Summary).

7. Quoted by Daneshkhu, S. (2016) 'UK farms face labour shortage as migrant workers pick elsewhere.' *Financial Times*, 9 December, 2016.

8. National Farmers Union. (2017) 'Access To A Competent And Flexible Workforce.' Accessed 12 September 2017 at https://www.nfuonline.com/news/eu-referendum

9. Rowthorn, R. (2015) *The Costs and Benefits of Large-scale Immigration*. London: Civitas.

10. Ibid., p.76.

11. Ruhs, M. (2013) *The Price of Rights: Regulating International Labor Migration*. Princeton, NJ: Princeton University Press.

12. Milanovic, B. (2016) 'There is a trade-off between citizenship and migration.' *Financial Times*. 20 April, 2016.

13. Rodrik, D. (2011) *The Globalization Paradox: Democracy and the Future of the World Economy*. Oxford: Oxford University Press.

14. Collier, P. (2013) *Exodus: How Migration is Changing Our World*. Oxford: Oxford University Press.

4

On the Promise and the Limits of Politics

Faith-based Responses to Asylum Seeking

Anna Rowlands, Durham University

The idea of a person's being a thing is a logical contradiction. Yet what is impossible in logic becomes true in life, and the contradiction lodged within the soul tears it to shreds.[1]

We are struggling to know what to do with how we relate to those we think of as strangers. So much so that this has become a central – and surprisingly tricky to grapple with – focus for our politics.

The 2016 Brexit campaign was dominated by concerns about tensions in our relations with strangers. Farage's billboard presenting the supposed hoards at Europe's borders was the nadir moment in a brittle debate haunted by the spectre of borders. In 2016 the idea of the border became paramount to our politics.

When invoked, these questions of the border and the role of the stranger are rarely ever simply about the question of our relation to foreigners. Brexit and the General Election of 2017 was a debate about borders *ad intra* and *ad extra*: a matter that concerned the relations within and between our communities as much as between our national community and it's perceived Other.

Such debates are also perhaps about the fissures within ourselves: the 'Anywhere' / 'Somewhere' (to invoke Goodhart[2]) agonies that lie within – not just between – souls. What is perceived to be broken is not merely a set of mutual ties between human beings divided by nationality, religion or race, rather we are left confronting the self–other relation at the heart of British society, a desire for its naming and – in however distorted a way – a seeking after its just repair. What we enacted in 2016 was a political self-relation as well as a self–other relation of some complexity that was long in the making, and which we are only just beginning to comprehend.

This chapter is written as a reflection on both trends in the politics of immigration stretching over several decades and as reflection on the summer of 2017, which I spent conducting interviews with the Jesuit Refugee Service in London. It is not intended as a comprehensive, exhaustive or summative account of the challenges we face in thinking about immigration in the UK. It presents no more than a partial truth about the state we are in. As such, it is a contribution to a necessary conversation we are trying and often failing to have as families, institutions, cities, regions and nations about immigration and the common good.

The purpose of this chapter is to pose the question: if politics is about both enacting the good and restraint of – or resistance to – what is evil, then what is the 'good' that we imagine an immigration and asylum system should serve and what is the harm that we are obliged to protect each other and the corporate social body from? These are posed as shared questions. Both questions, I suggest, are rooted in the ethical question of mutual obligations. Of course, to ask this question is already to frame the system in the context of an aspiration to shared value, shared language – what we might call after St Augustine the search to name common objects of love.

To frame things in this way does not always sit easily with current public policy making, but it is necessary for any serious consideration of a Christian social perspective. I do not answer this question in summary form, for the public conversation out of which a truly transformative account of migration and the common good might emerge is yet to take place. Rather I aim to shed light upon some of the possible substance of this conversation via the insights of those who have experienced the asylum system and through bringing to mind the deeper history of virtue mediated into the present through the texts and practices that constitute the Christian social tradition. I argue that in our public policy we are enacting a public forgetfulness about the necessary tasks or 'goods' of human government, while simultaneously failing to grasp the limits of politics. In both cases this is to displace the human person and the obligations that lie between us from the heart of our ethical reasoning. This is a forgetfulness that might also be a self-forgetting, and therefore echoing the striking imagery of Simone Weil in her meditation on the as a poem of force risks turning us all to stone.

Migration as a Christian social theme

Over the past decade the theme or issue of immigration has become increasingly significant for Christian social thought. Migration is incontrovertibly a defining generational question. It is also a question and an experience that suffuses the canon of Jewish and Christian writings. It is embedded in the narrative of Genesis, Leviticus, Joshua, Judges, Isaiah, the Psalms, Jeremiah, Ezekiel, Ezra-Nehemiah, Esther, Ruth, Acts, and 1 Peter to name but the most obvious texts. The Bible is self-evidently a history of migration and it proposes various political theologies of migration to its readers. Its texts are littered with figures that are caught up in, contribute towards, initiate, and attempt to redeem situations of migration and exile. Migration is presented to the reader of biblical texts as both a calling to a journey of blessings and a form of curse, a path through which God acts to redeem communities and establish his sovereignty, and a form of pathlessness, a form of obedience and disobedience to authorities of various kinds.

In common with other forms of complex narrative text, the Scriptures both reveal and hide from view those who are caught in the movement and the stasis that typifies migrations ancient and modern. In sum, the Scriptures represent a contested tradition of reflection on migration with insights that don't yield themselves to us as simply as we might first suppose.

It is also worth noting from the outset that Christian social reflection on migration in the English-speaking world emerging over the past decade has been written largely from the perspective of the so-called 'host' community and tends to be written drawing on biblical norms or wider deontological ethics. These are necessary and valuable perspectives, but they do not exhaust all that might be said. Here I draw briefly on metaphysical traditions in Christian social thought. These categories have resonance for public policy making, the narratives of those who find themselves negotiating the UK asylum system and the experiences of faith-based organisations who exist as bearers of an increasingly disruptive form of civic virtue in a highly contested and often toxic social context. I cannot claim to speak from the perspective of forced migrants, for this is not my experience. What I hope to do is to render the voices of my interviewees as a contribution to a wider social conversation and to reflect on their contribution in the light of my own tradition of Catholic social thought and my position as a member of a host community that bears responsibilities, exists within the ties of mutual obligation and deploys power.

Context: Jesuit Refugee Service

The purpose of my fieldwork with the Jesuit Refugee Service was to understand the position of asylum seekers who experience destitution and detention during, and in some instances following, the course of their seeking legal recognition in the UK and to reflect on the role of faith-based organisations in offering material, emotional and spiritual support in this context. The Jesuit Refugee Service (JRS) is an international Catholic organisation with a mission to accompany, serve and advocate on behalf of refugees and other forcibly displaced persons. JRS in the UK has a ministry to those who find themselves destitute as a consequence of government policies and those detained for the administration of immigration procedures. JRS UK runs a day centre, various educational, cultural and spiritual activities, a hosting scheme to provide accommodation for up to three months (called At Home), and detention outreach services to Heathrow IRC.

In a public context where most conversation about migration is reduced to the economic or political, to understand the role of JRS is to grasp that the debate about migration is always also both cultural and implicitly or explicitly theological. There is a shorthand tendency in current debate to oppose the categories of the social and economic (assumed to be the focus of liberals and cosmopolitans) to the cultural, where the 'cultural' position is understood to refer to legitimate concerns of social conservatives about the impact of immigration on values. In fact, the terrain of the 'cultural' and of values turns out to be well-populated and marked by a complexity and plurality of responses, responses that intersect with deeper traditions of thought and action that do not divide neatly into liberal or conservative viewpoints and which are mediated through religious and political traditions, the arts and so forth. The values question – indeed the value question – is irrupting again in our politics in contradictory and plural ways, the preserve of no one tradition or social group, cacophonous but certainly viscerally present. Each constituency seems to feel that its own values perspective is, variously, vital, contested, sometimes unwelcome or just indigestible in a public sphere marked by questions of interest rather than of value, and marked by fragility.

My fieldwork conducted during the summer of 2017 involved three weeks of visits to the Jesuit Refugee Service centre in Wapping, East London. I spent a week participating in the work of the centre, including the focal point of the week – a day centre that provides for around 100 men and women living in destitution. I undertook two further visits during which I conducted seventeen semi-structured interviews and six unstructured staff conversations. The aim of these interviews was to understand how people become destitute and how those refused asylum negotiate the process of living in constant interaction with the idea and concrete reality of the border. For some this meant lives in and out of immigration detention, for others lengthy periods of street homelessness and instability.

Castles and Miller define an asylum seeker as a person who 'has crossed an international border in search of protection, but whose claim for refugee status has not yet been decided'.[3] This is a sociological not a legal category, nonetheless its creation reinforces the transitory state experienced by forced migrants. By definition it is a transitional category, conveys a condition of impermanence and the notion of a process of contestation or claim and potential counter-claim. Well over half of those who claim asylum are rejected at the point of making a first claim. Having been issued with a refusal, those claiming asylum lose access to accommodation and are required to leave the UK within 21 days, or risk forced removal. The high rate of successful appeals gives some clue as to the inherent problems with the claims process as it currently stands, nonetheless many remain trapped within an extended period of waiting either between or beyond various stages of the legal process.

The Joseph Rowntree Foundation defines destitution as follows: 'lacking the means to meet the basic needs of shelter, warmth, food, water and health'.[4] The literature on destitution makes clear that asylum destitution is a condition that is consciously created by the state as part of its border management and deterrence strategy. Withdrawal of accommodation and privation of welfare support, refusal of work and detention are used as deliberate methods of deterrence and expulsion or of border control. Destitution amongst asylum seekers is largely driven by the following factors: the low level of initial successful applications for asylum at first hearing resulting in protracted appeals processes, the prohibition on paid work during a claim or appeals process, and the lack of access to reliable legal support. Policies of detention and dispersal also feed into dynamics that facilitate social isolation, increase – some would argue manufacture – vulnerability and therefore increase the risk of destitution and magnify its impact. My interviewees also identified poor casework and a disjointed and bureaucratic system that defies comprehension as contributing or aggravating factors. JRS identifies the housing rules that prevent asylum seekers being able to live in permanent non-rented or independently rented accommodation and apply for subsistence, the perverse incentives of Section 4 (soon to become 95A) requirements and difficulties in accessing healthcare as further factors in the production of destitution. For my research participants, destitution is enacted as a deliberate policy agenda – it is not an accidental, chosen or simply tragic status.

For those living through stages of refusal in an asylum application survival happens through a variety of routes – civil society organisations that provide day centres, night shelters, hosting schemes, legal services, toiletries and other essential provisions; reliance on informal arrangements for accommodation with friends or acquaintances – sometimes (out of desperation) in exchange for childcare, sexual or other domestic services. My research highlighted strongly gendered dynamics to survival in this situation, with women feeling especially vulnerable in public spaces. Spending the night moving between long-distance night buses as places of perceived relative safety, one interviewee described her choices carefully: 'I choose between two or three different night buses that go a long distance so I can sleep for an hour or so at a time, but going to destinations that I think are safer areas for changing buses.' 'You feel worthless and unwanted...but the bus feels safer to me, as a woman, than the streets.'

Just as unsatisfactory as sleeping on the street were some forms of 'hospitality' offered by friends or associates, with various forms of exploitation or indignity being described. In this context, the night shelters and hosting schemes offered by (often but not always) faith-based organisations are seen as a welcome, if far from ideal, option.

Trends in public policy

The gradual move towards the widespread or systematic deployment of destitution and detention as forms of border management dates to the policy shifts of the 1990s. The Asylum and Immigration Appeals Act of 1993 gave the Home Office the power to detain asylum seekers *prior* to making a decision on their case and also set a time limit for appeals. Further legislation in 1996 and 2002 – amongst a slew of recent Immigration Acts – placed restrictions on the right to paid work and eventually prohibited paid work completely. The 1999 Immigration and Asylum Act created for the first time a system of parallel but inferior welfare support for those seeking asylum. Placing the welfare of asylum seekers under the National Asylum Support Service (NASS), the Act created a new system of support tied to compliance with being accommodated in dispersed regional housing, removing a right to rent or stay with friends or relatives. Such housing was chosen on the basis that it was cheap and in areas with housing surplus. This system created a form of forced internal migration within the UK that was unwelcome and distressing to many because of the isolation and fracturing it brought with it. Many dispersal areas lacked the hyper-diversity that asylum seekers represented and had little or no civic or social preparation for the arrival of a new community of strangers. The strategy appeared to be driven both by economic considerations and by the move towards the deliberate manufacture of an increasingly 'hostile environment' (as Theresa May would come to express it) for asylum seekers as well as a kind of dismissal of the needs of local communities in dispersal areas. However, equally important to note according to one of my interviewees, is that the shift in legislation was accompanied by a breakdown in a wider communicative process between policy makers and sector professionals. One sector worker with more than 30 years' experience explained that he could recall a period under the late Thatcher government when it was still possible to have 'sensible discussions with Home Office people and with ministers'. Arguing that the end of the Cold War, coinciding with easier travel and domestic shifts contributed to a shift in mentality, he notes: 'it wasn't inherently hostile. There were some kinds of shared value and some shared language. You could negotiate on the basis of value for money or even the justice of the provision. The trump card of the sector is values. And we suddenly realised [in the 1990's] they didn't want to hear this'. This is an insight of some significance for understanding shifts in culture.

These are not simply trends that represent a failure of imagination in the UK, however. British public policy typifies a wider set of trends. Recent studies of European, Australian and North American public policy responses to forced migration have emphasised a significant shift in the way in which liberal nation states exercise state sovereignty forced migrants.[5] These include a move towards the intensification in the use of powers of detention and forced expulsion by the state; a move towards the exercise of migration control functions at sea, in detention centres and in offshore handling facilities; and the use of legislative power to create new restrictions on welfare and legal provision. This last change means that destitution becomes a form of border enforcement, such that both systems of welfare and law are marshalled more towards maximising levels of deterrence and expulsion than positive justice. The incremental decision to move towards detention used on a large scale has also produced an increasingly substantial private sector profit-making detention industry funded by the public purse. Immigration detention is a major growth industry in Europe and the US, as yet unaccompanied by any evident ethical reflection on the role of the private sector in the management of borders.

The use of immigration detention for administrative purposes has been a feature of European public policy since the 1970s, although the growth of detention as a serious form of border control dates from the 1990s and 2000s in most European countries. During this period detention has been used primarily as a mechanism for enforcing deportations and for responding to perceived security concerns. However, over the past decade there has been a significant shift towards the use of administrative detention as both a basic form of so-called reception of arriving migrants and as a form of overt immigration deterrence. It represents a complex form of social messaging.

If Southern and Eastern Europe provide examples of some of the most unregulated and draconian detention practices, then the UK provides an example of some of the most extensively and routinely used powers of detention deployed over four decades. In the UK we have held the power to detain immigrants for administrative purposes since 1971. However, this power was little used, and was introduced partly on that understanding. In 1993, 22 years after the creation of this power, there were just 250 bed spaces in the UK for immigrants to be detained. At the beginning of 2015 that number had risen dramatically to 3,915 bed spaces for any given night. Thus in the UK we are now routinely detaining 32,000 plus migrants a year in ten detention centres in England and Scotland for periods which range from a few days to several years.[6]

Most of those who are detained in the UK are either asylum applicants being processed through the so-called fast track process (a process recently ruled illegal by the High Court), visa over-stayers, those who are undocumented or stateless, or those who have served a prison sentence for arriving with a forged passport or irregular papers. Torture survivors and children are not supposed to be detained, although there is significant evidence that both categories are routinely detained. In the UK there is currently no limit on the amount of time a migrant may be detained – the only Western EU country where this is the case. The European limit is generally between 21 and 28 days, although there has been a shift towards enacting judicially approved detention for up to 18 months in cases where third country paperwork cannot be obtained. In the UK a number of current detainees have been incarcerated for over four years. The general trend is towards increased use of detention as a tool of border management, and an overall increase in the duration of detention. The last year has seen a two-thirds increase in those being held for more than a year in indefinite detention. This figure is all the more concerning when we note that the error rate in asylum cases remains at around 60 per cent and that of those detained only around 40 per cent go on to be removed from the UK, the remaining 60 per cent are returned from detention to the community, many of whom go on to receive legal status.[7] On the available evidence it seems fair to conclude that detention has been normalised as an institutional response to migration in the UK.

To begin to talk about detention in this statistical and more abstract manner is, however, to risk evading a central paradox concerning what is and is not visible in the case of immigration detention.[8] While state structures form a kind of panoptic culture – immigration management through the formulation of new disciplinary institutions – detention is a practice that the state prefers not to discuss and wishes to keep as a space of both hyper-surveillance and yet invisibility. The geographical isolation of centres, limited access to sites and legal challenges to freedom of information requests speak to this reality. Migrants are typically moved into centres through the use of dawn raids and frequently moved between centres at night. Centres are often located in places of low public visibility. During the course of my research my first interviewee was detained in a raid on her accommodation late at night and threatened with deportation two days later. In the event, some kind of administrative error on the part of the centre or Home Office seems to have resulted in the charter flight taking off without her on board and a protracted period in another detention centre.

The intended invisibility of detention is starting to be challenged by some ground-breaking academic studies and policy reports that offer empirical insights into the nature of detainee experiences. Such work reveals acutely the disconcerting ways in which the contemporary use of detention represents something deeply troubling in the practice of the state. An example of this is the 2015 UK cross-party parliamentary report on immigration detention.[9] The report – the first of its kind in the UK – is based on hearings with detainees, Home Office representatives as well as various legal and medical professionals.

Those giving testimony argue that detention produces in its detainees a condition akin to – but also unlike – that of prisoners. One detainee describes the extreme distorting effect detention has on perceptions of time: 'In prison you count your days down, but in detention you count your days up.'[10] A medical doctor who frequently visits detention facilities describes this same phenomenon:

> *By being detained indefinitely, without knowing how long for and with the continual possibility of both immanent release and removal, detainees worry that detention will continue forever and also that it will end in unexpected deportation the next morning. They have the simultaneous concern both that there will be sudden change and never-ending stasis. It is the lack of temporal predictability that prevents … individuals not only from being able to plan for the future, but also from having the ability of knowing that the present will remain uncertain for a protracted length of time.[11]*

The compression of time, generation of fear, and the atomisation of social experience are all hallmarks of detention. In my own conversations at JRS a visceral fear of detention marked interviews both with those who had been detained and with those who hadn't but feared it nonetheless. For those who had been detained the experience was marked by a sense of dispossession and loss, a permanent diminution.

> *Detention finishes people off. It's a form of mental trauma that takes away skill and capacity. We see this in people who have been highly skilled before – doctors, dentists, nurses, university*

teachers, but who can't function in these roles even when they later achieve status, because they never fully recover from the trauma of detention.

In all my interviews the trauma of detention was connected to the use of force, the absence of a time limit and the mimicking of a criminal justice process (but without process) that conveys the idea of a criminal act or intent that detainees cannot internalise or own as a self-identity.

Detention is a context that denies love. Staff can be nice but the problem is the use of force, which shapes the whole reality. The system tells you (in all its actions) that you are an identity that you cannot accept.

You know you are there because you aren't believed. The culture of disbelief re-traumatises already traumatised people.

When we know that there are alternatives, we know it is wrong.

But the ripples of detention and its 'messaging' were felt more widely, most acutely when my interviewees went to report at Home Office facilities. 'Every time I went to report I felt sick. You know you might not come out again.'

In the hosting scheme one religious sister said she was shocked to discover that their destitute guest carried with her each time she left the house, for any purpose, a bag packed with all her belongings, just in case she was detained. One interviewee uses military language to describe how he sees the 'messaging' of detention:

It's shock and awe tactics. It's about the message of fear, that all is but a stay of execution – the sudden detention of one person is meant as a message to the rest of us… It's about fear and power.

It aims to maximise your sense of insecurity and fear. I think the Home Office know what they are doing.

Time, or temporality, emerges as a key moral theme not only in interviewees and reports about the impact of immigration detention but also in discussions of the impact of destitution. One interviewee told me that destitution is experienced as just as damaging as detention, because it also distorts healthy experiences of inhabiting time. He described both the trauma of inhabiting an open-ended time of waiting – never knowing how long he would be in this situation – but also an acutely agonising awareness of the passing of time.

This was a theme repeated across my interviews. Part of the suffering that the system causes is an acute awareness of time passing, or wasting time. 'Waiting, reporting, not working, the manner of treatment – sometimes in charities as well as by the Home Office or lawyers – dehumanises. It destroys us. Destitution makes us go mad.' 'Without structure you become susceptible to lots of things: isolation, criminality, addiction, mental and physical illnesses.' Others used the striking and disturbing image of physical decomposition to express their experience of destitution: 'I feel as if I am degrading.'

A repeated insight was that the experience of destitution and its attendant stresses had led to a permanent loss of skills and capacity and thus a fundamental loss of a sense of selfhood – a permanent form of dispossession. One woman who had been a nurse in her country of origin said,

Previously, I was a nurse. But the asylum process traumatised me. I'm not the same person now. So much time was killed. I can't go back to what I did before. I suffer with heart problems now. I never had those before I came here, even with all the trauma that happened to me back home.

Referring with distress to a friend, I was told, 'He was a [health care professional] in his country. But he will never be able to function again like this here I don't think. He has waited too long. He is too unwell now.'

Another woman who spent many months sleeping on night buses explained that the chronic sleep deprivation meant that she could feel a sense of her capacity drain away; 'How old will I be when this is sorted? My ability is already not the same. I could have done so much in this country before. But now? I'm trying so hard to be normal.' This woman, a 40-year-old survivor of extreme sexual violence and torture in her country of origin notes how, in living so many years waiting for an outcome and without access to resources, 'the two halves of life come to feel like they repeat the same thing'.

Another woman explained the impact of the lack of nutritious food available to her:

> *There are no nutritious things going inside me. The doctor told me he was fed up of seeing me coming in with food poisoning from the effects of eating food that had gone out of date. The system shapes everything. My dream is stability and study to be a midwife but I don't think my brain could take in the study now. Even things I could do before, I am too tired to do.*

Repeatedly I was told that the system generates hopelessness. On the one hand, this hopelessness relates to the stasis of the system and its non-responsiveness. On the other hand, it relates to what a number of interviewees describe as the disciplinary structure of the system. One interviewee described the way that the system feels like it quite deliberately aims to foster a self-identity in the asylum claimant that is the opposite to those that enabled flight: 'fleeing takes enterprise, courage, determination, judgement. We see ourselves as having these characteristics. But the system creates a sense of ourselves as the opposite of these things'. 'The system makes us in its own image.'

Interviewees describe the sense that the system increases rather than limits the sense of dependence on others or the sense that one is vulnerable and a drain on other people. Interviewees asked me 'where else in the policy system would such non-preventative policies be enacted?' With some anger another asylum seeker argued 'they want to shape the image and shape of asylum seekers. You want to make a particular kind of community, with asylum seekers shaped in that image. The limits you place on us – on pursuing what is important to us, to being human – are about seeking to destroy something'. She continued: 'The system shapes your life – especially as a woman – in such a way that it means you live with no love, no life. Relationships require stability. The system ensures that I have no stability.'

Reframing contributive justice

For others it is important that we reflect on the social context of the denial of contribution – particularly the absence of a right to work – faced by asylum seekers. One interviewee expressed his case as follows:

> *A capitalist system values the idea of contribution. You need to contribute to get something out – when you are not contributing (in the way society understands contribution) you don't feel like a member of society. This is deliberate, they [the Home Office] know what they are doing ... This isn't just a form of social death but also intellectually you suffer and die because you can't engage, participate or contribute. People don't take this into account when thinking about destitution and what the asylum system sets out to do, but it's crucial to understand.*

A sector specialist interviewed for my research echoed the sense that the messaging that public policy is involved in is a complex form of social communication:

The hostile environment functions not by being enforceable but by sending a message. Whether it's sending a message to the electorate, to the media, or actually to migrants themselves is unclear ... but the messaging of it is where the power lies. And that is part of the danger around the hostile environment policies – it is that the people who are most likely to hear are not the direct targets. It is heard, and its effects felt, not by those...who are forced into precarious situations as a result ... but it sets the context to their life.

I asked my participants what changes they would most like to see made to the asylum system. Their answers were various, however in all cases they included three core assertions: the right to work while cases are being heard and a time limit for immigration detention and better quality of – and more accountable – casework. Other advocacy requests included improvements to the transition arrangements so that the asylum system and integration into work systems for those who gain refugee status work in a coherent way.

One interviewee had thought hard about the application of Catholic social thought to the asylum system. He told me that he would use the principle of subsidiarity to restructure the system. He argued that decision-making should be decentralised and operate with some regional autonomy, that casework should be tailored to individual needs and the many layers of subcontracting reviewed as they mitigate against efficiency and humanity.

Beyond the story of the suffering victim

Understanding the impact of the asylum system should not, however, lead us to the conclusion that passive suffering defines all that might be said about the experience of my interviewees. Those negotiating lives lived along an ever-present border also speak of spaces and places that have been transformative for them and which they have contributed to the transformation of – spaces that constitute the very opposite of the distortion of time that they associate with the asylum system.

Typical of responses I received, one interviewee told me that JRS is a counter-culture within the asylum system partly because it facilitates 'time well spent' in the face of the degrading of time. What is time well spent? 'Being active, providing a service to others, food, conversation, mutual assistance, meeting people who are different to you and hearing their stories, sharing experience, comforting one another; all these enable perseverance. Time well spent is finding ways to keep going.' 'What makes you feel human is doing something gainful for yourself whilst helping others who are going through their own struggles, and being recognised by others as a person.'

Identifying hospitable spaces was a crucial theme. On the one hand, hospitable spaces were those that provided for public engagement and recognition without fostering anxiety or shame, for example the day centre service at JRS. The fact that day centre attendees are addressed by name, greeted by hand, that staff eat their food alongside guests is crucial for identifying this space as hospitable. What this environment created was a sense of dignified kinship, a sensibility stripped away by the process of claiming status. 'I wanted to be with people who could respect me.' 'Being with people who respect you enables you – despite all the stress – to see that maybe there is another side to your story that you don't yet know.'

Another interviewee explained 'the system makes you feel… well…you don't feel considered, don't feel part of a world or a real system. I come here and I feel like I have a family, that I am part of a world.' 'The way you are treated here is like the opposite of how you are treated everywhere else in the system. It's basic things that make the difference: a warm welcome, they use your name, shake your hand, eat food with you, view you as human. This kind of interaction is what provides emotional support for me.'

The same interviewee explained that he no longer attended day centres where the staff did not eat alongside their refugee guests. However, others also talked about a counterbalancing need for creating places of privacy in which they were not expected to interact.

For some, public libraries represented such spaces: 'No one looks at you. You can spend as much time as you like there. It gives you a kind of privacy. Because I don't have any private space, this becomes my place of privacy.'

The experience of faith – understood not simply as personal belief but as membership of communities of thought and practice – emerged as a key factor amongst my participants. I asked no direct question about religion or faith but in all but one instance my interviewees told me that it had been the major sustaining factor for them; it had enabled perseverance and resilience.

For some, faith had been challenged during this experience. One interviewee told me: 'People assume coming from outside the UK that the justice system in the UK is based on Christian values. The Queen is the head of the Church of England and swearing oaths on the Bible etc. But the way that you experience the system doesn't feel like this. [It's] confusing and this can have an impact on your faith too. The system is seen by people like me as a faith-based system that has let them down. In a Christian society, why a system that is so unjust?'

For some, faith had given them hope that 'God has a plan for me and that plan is good.' For others, the Scriptures had offered them a language through which to make sense of the contradictions of their experience: 'like the Psalms say, I have walked through the valley of death and I know what it is like, but I also know that God was with me. This was my experience. Both things are true'.

Others describe the importance of feeling that they are part of a community of others: 'There are times when things are overwhelming and I couldn't pray. But the prayer of the community enabled my spirit to be lifted up.'

In some cases those interviewed described in fairly classic Christian language a process of de-centring of the self and in some cases dramatic conversion. Reshaping the insight that the core ethical concern should be with time and temporality one former detainee interviewee told me, 'What matters is not time but promise.' He narrated the story of Abraham and Sarah to me as an example of God's intervention in the normal processes of time to enable the wellbeing of his people. 'Grace transforms how we experience time. God makes [Sarah] fertile in old age. This is unmerited grace. This is God's promise.' He explained how he had preached this message in the chapel of his detention centre and believed he had saved the life of a suicidal fellow detainee in the process.

While all interviewees recognised the humanising qualities of JRS and its contrast to their experience in the asylum system, many were also clear that JRS exists within that system; it does not fully transcend the reality of the asylum process. 'Not knowing your future is very difficult. You feel like a dead person walking, not yourself anymore, depressed and anxious all the time. You are living a different life, living in a different world to everyone else. Eating only in day centres, no accommodation. It is a hard life. A difficult life.'

Key to the way that JRS works is that it enables asylum seekers without status to act as volunteers. In a context where paid work is not possible the option to volunteer and be recognised as a person with skills and capacities was greatly valued. Many talk about the way that this reverses temporarily the sense of time wastage, combats the stress that comes with enforced idleness and builds relationships that help to overcome isolation. It enables a sense of contributive justice not bound tightly to the dominant socio-economic order identified by my previous interviewee. Others talk about building new skills and a new perspective, with the diversity they encounter being a key point of ethical learning for them. 'You learn more about what you are capable of.' 'It made me a more curious person.' 'It has helped me build more compassion.' 'It has enabled me to receive love.'

Conceiving of these roles also enables a service that meets the needs of asylum seekers in a more holistic sense. 'Being myself a refugee, having been an asylum seeker, waiting with others... I can give them more confidence. Because I've been in their shoes...

I know when those shoes feel hot… I can *feel* what our friends say. This means I can help understand what's happening underneath.'

The promise of politics

Interviewees posed repeatedly one key rhetorical question: what is the purpose of this system? Who actually benefits? Drawing on their own experience they argue that its sole felt aim seems to be to discourage, to limit access to protection as part of a policy of deterrence, and to demarcate and discipline asylum seeking into acceptable and unacceptable forms. Several of my respondents also argued that they believed the system itself to be incapable of answering their question: that no stable answer could be given that represented the system as a whole, that one part of the system could not coherently answer the question in the light of another. That the policies they were subject to seemed to defy any sensible conception of politics as the pursuit of the good mattered hugely to those to whom I spoke.

Augustine's notion of evil outlined in his Confessions – and in repudiation of Manichean belief – holds that evil is without substance, a negation or privation of being and goodness.[12] What is evil does not have being in itself but rather is parasitic on what is and what is good. As such evil exists – metaphysically speaking – as a form of non-being. The claim that evil is a form of non-being should not be confused with a proposition that evil is an illusion nor a claim that evil is felt in empirical terms as anything other than the deepest of agonies. Rather Augustine's claim for evil as non-being forms the basis of a case that evil can only meaningfully be thought of as residing in a disordered good. Rowan Williams narrates Augustine's argument thus:

> *If evil itself is never a subject or substance, the only way in which it can be desired or sought is by the exercise of the goods of mental and affective life swung around by error to a vast misapprehension, a mistaking of the unreal and groundless for the real. The more such a pursuit continues, the more the desiring subject becomes imprisoned, enslaved, hemmed in; the more*

the typical excellences of the will and intelligence are eroded.
However, that does not mean that the effects of this nightmare
error are lessened.[13]

Here Williams expounds Augustine's view that sin and evil gain
their force not merely as a move from focusing on higher to
lower goods, but through a continual process in which the good
(and what is evil) is misrecognised, and embedded as a lack of
the good through the force of habit.[14] What we experience as
evil therefore is not so much *a lack* but the *effect* of a lack, 'the
[habitual] displacement of true by untrue perception'.[15] In Book
VII of the *Confessions* Augustine emphasises a repeated theme in
his theology: that a failure to grasp the good and a willingness to
fall into evil manifests an improper or distorted form of seeing:
a distorted visualisation of God, and a distorted visualisation of
ourselves as human creatures.

It is hard not to listen to my interviewees and feel that they are
describing in the starkest and most ordinary terms a public policy
process in which the good is lost, a good that is both public and
individual and therefore also common. Augustine provides a
metaphysical language to challenge public policy makers to
account for the good that the current asylum framework provides,
and to do so in ways that connect the good of those whose lives are
dependent on that system and who are subject to its force and the
good of those who imagine their collective or common interests to
be protected through this system. Here, echoing my participants,
I make the case simply for raising this matter as a pressing moral
question that seems to lack coherent or convincing public answers.
Such an absence of lack implies a falling away from the promise
and task of politics itself.

The limits of politics

However, the work of JRS poses questions about the nature of
the political that exceed the question of the necessary focus
of public policy. In her essay on Homer's *Iliad* (which she reads
as a refugee poem) Simone Weil writes of the nature of force that

brutalises in the following way: force is the 'x that turns anybody who is subjected to it into a thing. Exercised to the limit, it turns man into a thing in the most literal sense: it makes a corpse out of him'. My participants described the ways in which they come to feel that force makes corpses out of them. This is not an overdramatic claim, it is a descriptive account of how the system can feel as well as a literal truth in some cases.

JRS exists within this system (not apart from it) as witness to its operations and as an internal counter-culture. It aims to counter the process through which social processes render us corpses, to raise the person to life. In acting as a counterpoint to the culture of disbelief JRS renders visible an important truth: that to be a host community or state does not necessarily imply the experience of hospitality, intended or received.

In fact, we might posit a current alienation or fundamental tension between these two notions. We might go further and argue that as public policy becomes gradually more hostile and restrictive for asylum seekers, hospitality is being reinvented within host nations as something of a counter-culture largely through civic networks.

This is not accidental. The moral imagination and traditions of Catholic social thought that undergird the practice of JRS emphasise a set of obligations that exist between human persons that precede and exceed the formation of nations and states. Christian social thought does and can make a contribution to public policy debate. But to say this fails to capture a second crucial role played by Christian social thought: the deconstruction of the idea that the state is 'all in all', even on a very good day. We can construct a deontological debate which is concerned with exactly how we balance our duty to different kinds of migrants (using categories we have created and refined for the purpose) and we can worry about how we balance rights and duties and how we encourage others to do the same, and we can imagine that this exhausts or settles the virtue question.

These are reasonable debates of course, but organisations like JRS trouble the idea that this constitutes the boundaries of the virtue debate. Instead, their work begs the basic human question of a messy pre-political space, of the unstable and contingent nature of the way we set border practices and deal with the consequences for bare human lives, and of the hierarchy of the social over the political.

This is the space in which those whose stories do not fit neat categories, or who find that power prevents them from accessing a justice that should be theirs can still find a space of mutuality. From a Christian point of view this is a space of mutual human obligation that the political ought not to colonise, but which many faith-based organisations feel is shrinking and becoming increasingly politicised. If the testimony of asylum seekers confronts us with the failure of government to live up to the promise of politics, then the associational work of JRS confronts us with our lamentable failure to abide by the necessary limit of politics.

The specifics of this consideration of the condition of the asylum system are not intended as a technical discussion of a narrow area of public policy. Rather, the questions and insights of my interviewees point to a wider set of challenges for a post-Brexit politics. Arguably, the turn to post-liberalism and populism (in its various, plural and fast changing guises) while offering interesting perspectives on the renewal of community, a reformed capitalism and a new political settlement seems to struggle quite profoundly with the place of the stranger or non-citizen who addresses us from within and outside our borders as fellow human beings. This remains a profound challenge to the next generation of political theorists, activists and leaders.

ENDNOTES

1. Weil, S. (2005) 'The Iliad or the Poem of Force.' In *Simone Weil: An Anthology*. London: Penguin, p.188.

2. Goodhart, D. (2017) *The Road to Somewhere: The Populist Revolt and the Future of Politics*. London: Hurst.

3. Castles, S. B. and Miller, M.J. (2009) *The Age of Migration: International Population Movements in the Modern World*. 4th edition. Basingstoke: Palgrave Macmillan.

4. Fitzpatrick, S., Bramley, G., Sosenko, F., Blenkinsopp, J. et al. (2016) *Destitution in the UK*. London: Joseph Rowntree Foundation. Accessed October 2017 at https://www.jrf.org.uk/report/destitution-uk

5. Gibney, M. (2008) 'Asylum and the Expansion of Deportation in the United Kingdom.' *Government and Opposition*, 43, 2; Home Office. (2005) *Controlling our Borders: Making Migration Work for Britain*. London: Home Office.

6. For a legal overview of detention, see Wilsher, D. (2012) *Immigration Detention: Immigration Detention: Law, History, Politics*. Cambridge: Cambridge University Press. This chapter engages in particular with the (currently unparalleled) in-depth UK ethnographic work of Bosworth, M. (2014) *Inside Immigration Detention*. Oxford: Oxford University Press. See also the All Party Parliamentary Group on Refugees and the All Party Parliamentary Group on Migration, The Report of the Inquiry into the Use of Immigration Detention in the United Kingdom, March 2015, available at https://detentioninquiry.files.wordpress.com/2015/03/immigration-detention-inquiry-report.pdf (accessed 03/2017).

7. 'The Report of the Inquiry into the Use of Immigration Detention in the United Kingdom: A Joint Inquiry by the All Party Parliamentary Group on Refugees & the All Party Parliamentary Group on Migration.' Accessed 30 November 2017 at https://detentioninquiry.files.wordpress.com/2015/03/immigration-detention-inquiry-report.pdf

8. See Schmid-Scott, A. (2016) 'Reimagining violence: Hannah Arendt and the bureaucratisation of life in immigration detention.' Unlocked UK. Accessed March 2017 at http://unlocked.org.uk/blog/reimagining-violence-hannah-arendt-and-the-bureaucratisation-of-life-in-immigration-detention

9. Immigration Detention Inquiry Report.

10. Ibid., p.18.

11. Ibid., p.19.

12. St. Augustine. (1961) *Confessions*. London: Penguin. Book VII, pp.12, 13, 16.

13. Williams, R. (2015) 'Insubstantial Evil.' In *On Augustine*. London: Bloomsbury, p.88.

14. On move from higher to lower goods see St. Augustine. (1961) *Confessions*. London: Penguin. Book VII, 16. See also Russell, F.H. (1990) '"Only Something Good Can be Evil": The Genesis of Augustine's Secular Ambivalence.' *Theological Studies* 51, 4. See also Prendeville, J.G. (1972)

'The Development of the Idea of Habit in the Thought of Saint Augustine.' *Traditio*, 28. Both referenced in David Grumett, 'Arendt, Augustine and Evil.' *Heythrop Journal*, 2000, pp.154-169.

15. Williams, R. (2015) 'Insubstantial Evil.' In *On Augustine*. London: Bloomsbury.

5

Biblical and Theological Perspectives on Migration

Susanna Snyder, University of Roehampton

The traveling self is here both the self that moves physically from one place to another, following 'public routes and beaten tracks' within a mapped movement; and the self that embarks on an undetermined journeying practice, having constantly to negotiate between home and abroad, native culture and adopted culture, or more creatively speaking, between a here, a there, and an elsewhere.[1]

To be rooted is perhaps the most important and least recognised need of the human soul.[2]

Biblical texts – from Genesis to Revelation – are imbued with experiences of and responses to migration, and in recent years, increasing flows of people across borders and political debate around immigration have left an imprint on theology more broadly. Theologians have sought to grapple with this global and also inherently local and regional phenomenon and its human consequences in a variety of sending and receiving countries, and in relation to migrants who are categorised in law and policy in different ways – not least because many migrants inhabit a religious tradition and because faith-based organisations have been at the forefront of responses to those crossing borders.[3] In this chapter, I present a smorgasbord of biblical and theological perspectives on migration, focusing on how these might inform receiving communities.

While making simplistic connections between religious texts written in a very different time and place and contemporary reality should be avoided, insight into perennial human experiences and socio-political dynamics can be gleaned. The Bible is a conversation among the people of God over centuries – people who grappled with issues similar to those we grapple with today, and who have sought to understand the call of God to them – and they do not always agree. The Bible does not present us with neat answers or directly applicable policy solutions. What the Bible does is invite us to enter into the experiences and debates of those who have gone before us, and to make a creative and imaginative response to our current situation in the light of their wisdom. It gives us an opportunity to hone our ethical sensibilities and sharpen our ability to make right moral judgements.[4]

In the process, what the Bible also invites us to do – and what this chapter will seek to do – is to keep human beings front and centre. Rather than abstract discussion of immigration as an *issue*, this chapter will engage with the embodied, messy experience of both migrants and members of established communities – and with the encounters between them. Through this, it hopes to highlight and diminish what geographer Nick Gill describes as the 'moral distance' that often exists between citizens in Western countries and migrants – a distance that allows Westerners to see migrants as alien and therefore deserving of little moral concern.[5] We need to avoid inhabiting the paradoxical trap that Edward Said pointed to when he wrote that mass migration was 'strangely compelling to think about but terrible to experience'.[6] I am writing self-consciously as a privileged white British citizen who, while having sought to stand alongside migrants for more than twelve years, knows how easy this trap is to fall into.

This chapter explores in particular the tension between two inherent aspects of human experience and identity – the call to be rooted in home, place and community and the call to move, to risk and to journey towards newness. Or, to put it differently, the apparent conflict between being embedded in a place and dwelling 'between a here, a there and an elsewhere'.[7] This tension lies at the heart of much political debate surrounding immigration today in Britain: are we a series of communities dug deep in locality and bound to those who are like us (and therefore likely to prioritise members of established communities over immigrants), or are we part of a cosmopolitan, global community whose identity and rights come from our common humanity? Are we, to use David Goodhart's terms, 'somewheres' or 'anywheres'?[8] As we will see, this tension is not simply one that the Bible fails to resolve: it is one that is seen as lying at the heart of what it means to be human. These two poles are not mutually exclusive.

Human beings as migrants, and migrants as human beings

The starting point for any discussion of migration in the Bible has to be that the people of God are migrants themselves. Being on the move is part of our identity as human beings, and the themes of strangeness, travel, journeying and uprooting weave their way through the Bible as a recurring thread. The Bible is written by and for people who understand themselves to be exiles, migrants and sojourners in their social and political contexts and in this world.

In the first few chapters of Genesis alone, Adam and Eve are displaced from the Garden of Eden after they eat the forbidden fruit (3.22–24), Cain is banished (4.12) and the people are scattered at Babel (11.8–9). The life of Abraham is one of journeying, uprooting and constant movement. Abraham gathers his family and possessions, and leaves his home in Haran to go to Shechem in response to a command from God (12.1) – a departure which has been described as 'wrenching'.[9]

From Shechem, he travels on to Bethel, Ai, the Negeb and Egypt. Abraham is referred to repeatedly using the Hebrew word *gēr*, which can loosely be translated as sojourner or resident alien. So, uprootedness suffuses the identity of the forefather of Judaism, Christianity and Islam. Hagar/Hājar, Sarah's Egyptian slave-girl who becomes Abraham's mistress and the mother of Ishmael/Ismā'īl, a significant figure for Muslims – becomes a forced migrant as she is cast out into the desert. She has to wander around as a nomad in the 'wilderness of Beer-sheba' (Genesis 16, 21.14).[10] Joseph was sold by his brothers to traffickers and found himself living as an alien slave in Egypt; and the Israelites wandered for 40 years in the wilderness on their way to the Promised Land.[11]

The exile – the forcible uprooting of members of the Judean community to Babylon following imperial conquest, first in 597 and then 586 BCE – was a trauma that defined much of what is written in the Bible. Those deported lost not just their homes, but also social status, wealth and family.[12] The experience of exile was the forge that produced the grief-stricken poetry of the Psalms and Lamentations; the prophetic books such as Isaiah and Jeremiah bewailing the conquest and deportation and trying to understand why it had happened; and indeed, the writing of the Torah – the first five books of the Bible – where the experience of movement is so central.[13]

Similar themes surface in the New Testament. Jesus fled to Egypt as a baby to escape Herod's death threats, and as an adult, described himself as someone who had no home with no place to lay his head (Luke 9.58; Mark 6.4). He lived at the edges of society, as a displaced person who disrupted conventional notions of space and place.[14] For Karl Barth, even the incarnation of Jesus was an example of migration – from the divine to humanity. It was God's way into the 'far country'.[15] The early Christians addressed each other as 'exiles' and 'aliens' in this world, and saw each other as strangers on their way to a heavenly home (e.g. 1 Peter 1; Hebrews 13.14).

In 1 Peter, written in Asia Minor in 73–92 CE, two words are used to self-describe the early Christians – *paroikos*, meaning foreign or 'other', and *parapidemos*, meaning transient visitor, pilgrim, sojourner. *Paroikos* was, significantly, a real socio-political category. It referred to people who inhabited the edges of Roman society, lacking the full belonging and rights of citizens (until the imperial adoption of Christianity by Constantine in around 312).

The late second- or early-third-century Christian document, *The Epistle of Diognetus*, summarises Christian self-understanding at this time: 'They live in their own countries, but only as aliens. They have a share in everything as citizens, and endure everything as foreigners… They busy themselves on earth, but their citizenship is in heaven.'[16] Travel was the key to the spreading of the gospel, and Paul is reputed to have travelled 10,000 miles on his missionary journeys to spread the gospel.[17]

Migration and movement are part of Islamic tradition too. The *hijra* or flight of the Prophet Mohammed from Mecca to Medina in 622 marked the beginning of the Muslim calendar, and the *Hajj* – an annual pilgrimage to Mecca – is one of five pillars of Islam that Muslims are expected to practice today.[18]

This said, home and dwelling are still seen as crucially important in biblical narratives. All of the movement people undertake is in pursuit of a home – a place to abide, to dwell, to inhabit and live fully and permanently – be that the Promised Land, or a heavenly home.[19] The Bible does not validate, commend or romanticise migration for its own sake, recognising that it carries considerable risks and is invariably costly. There is, instead, a constant see-sawing between the call to uproot and move, and the call to put down roots and to abide. As soon as the people of God become too comfortable and stuck in their ways or they experience injustice, they are deracinated and called to newness and transformative liberation; once they are on the move, God longs with them and accompanies them as they journey towards a new home and place to be at rest. Exile, displacement and being willing to be challenged and changed and to be on the outside are conditions that human beings cannot escape in their search for home.

Given that being a full human being involves movement and migration in some way, it should come as no surprise that theologians have sought to emphasise the full humanity of contemporary migrants. Every human being is created in the *imago dei* – the image of God – and movement (as well as dwelling) is part of that divine image (Genesis 1.26). As such, every migrant is deserving of dignity and respect. They should be engaged with as someone with a name and a story. Having equal worth, they are as equally entitled as those currently settled and living in stability to a level of rights and responsibilities that recognises their human dignity. This challenges much contemporary rhetoric which de-personalises and dehumanises migrants – including the use of words such as 'swarm,' 'flood', 'invasion' and 'illegal immigrants' in the tabloid press.

All too often, the humanity of those on the move is obscured in a morass of statistics, and those in receiving communities become anaesthetised to human pain in an abstract discussion of 'solutions' which assumes that migration is a theoretical puzzle to crack. When stories about refugees drowning appear in the news every day, they can barely touch the consciousness of those of us who are settled.

For many, refugees – and migrants more broadly – sit at the periphery of our vision as 'bare humanity' or 'bare life', devoid of the humanity that we have come to connect only in its fullest sense with citizenship of a national polity – and sometimes, only with citizenship of our own particular nation state.[20] And while migrants may travel without authorisation from a receiving country or documents recognised in a court of law, no human being is her/himself inherently illegitimate or unlawful. Migrants have become simultaneously both *invisible* – in that individuals are often hidden in high-fenced camps and detention centres and/or practice 'strategic invisibility' to evade deportation – and *hypervisible* – presented by the media in hyperbolic language as an undifferentiated mass threatening our way of life, resources and security.[21] Both invisibility and hypervisibility distort the humanity – *the imago dei* – present within individual migrants, making migrants both less and more than they are. Language and policy that associate immigrants with crime and illegality serve to create rather than simply exacerbate associations receiving populations make between newcomers and wrongdoing.

By contrast, what the Christian tradition calls those of us who are not currently migrating to do is to enter into the lives of migrants as human beings – individuals with names and faces who are loving and loved members of families, communities and societies – and to see ourselves in one another. I wonder what it might mean to stop thinking of ourselves as 'us' and migrants as 'them', and instead for us all to imagine ourselves together as a new 'we': a 'we' simultaneously on the move and seeking dwelling in a home?

Compassion and justice for the stranger – and solidarity

From the understanding that we are all, in some way, both migrants and dwellers emerges a call in the Christian tradition to respond to those migrating – especially those who are most vulnerable – with compassion, and to do so out of empathy. A constant refrain in the Bible is that a healthy and just community working for the flourishing of all demonstrates care and love for strangers and others who are marginalised.

Passages calling for care to be shown to the *gēr* (or *gerim* in the plural) – a sojourner or non-Israelite living in Israel – crop up throughout the Hebrew Bible. For example:

> *When an alien resides with you in your land, you shall not oppress the alien. The alien who resides with you shall be to you as the citizen among you: you shall love the alien as yourself, for you were aliens in the land of Egypt. (Leviticus 19.33–34)*

As former Chief Rabbi Jonathan Sacks noted, while there is only one verse in the Hebrew Bible demanding love of neighbour, we are invited to love the stranger 36 times.[22] Israelites and the *gerim* are to be treated fairly under the law, and have equal access to the six cities of sanctuary under Israelite jurisdiction designed to create a space for fugitives accused of murder to await trial rather than face direct vengeance (Joshua 20.9; Numbers 35.15).[23] Care and justice for the stranger and the existing resident are not seen as mutually incompatible.

Turning to the New Testament, we find again repeated calls for care to be shown towards those who are foreign or living at the edge of society. Jesus had an extensive ministry with those who were marginalised and distrusted by mainstream society – from those who were not Jewish to lepers and tax collectors. In the Parable of the Sheep and Goats (Matthew 25.31–46), Jesus tells a story about what will happen at the Last Judgement. He explains that those who feed the hungry, clothe the naked, give water to the thirsty, visit those in prison and welcome strangers will be saved – they are the sheep – while those who do not will face condemnation – they are the goats. Righteousness requires offering care to those considered 'the least' (25.40). In the letter to the Hebrews, the writer tells the early Christians: 'Do not neglect to show hospitality to strangers' (Hebrews 13.2). The Greek word used here for hospitality is *philoxenia*, which literally means love of foreigners or strangers – and significantly, *xenos* means both stranger and guest.

What does such care and hospitality mean in practice? First, it is about compassion – literally meaning suffering with – which starts with an encounter with migrants themselves, ideally in person or, if this is not possible, mediated through news coverage, the arts or other forms of storytelling. We need to enter into relationship with those migrating, allowing migrants' lived realities to pierce the self-preoccupations and numbness of those of us who are currently settled. Many migrants – while extraordinarily resilient and often hopeful against the odds – suffer physically, materially, psychologically and spiritually as they make journeys thousands of miles away from their homes.

Theologian Daniel Groody has referred to migration as a 'way of the cross'.[24] People frequently experience crucifixion – a series of little deaths and sometimes, real death – *en route* and after they arrive in a new place. Migration, for those with the fewest resources, represents a contemporary *via dolorous* (way of sorrow). Their feet burn with exhaustion and sores on a road of grief. In this context the call to compassion is a call to help carry the cross and to do all that we can to provide space, both literally and metaphorically, so that our fellow human beings can begin to rebuild their lives and flourish. Rather than simply grappling with migration as an issue at an intellectual level, we are called to turn our faces towards the faces of migrants so that we can connect with their humanity and enter into their pain.[25]

Second, offering care and hospitality needs to go beyond charity or niceness – or what is sometimes today called slacktivism – the kind of middle class cheque-book activism that is all too easy to do through sending a text message donation from the sofa. While charity and financial generosity remain important, we need also to work for a more just and fair global migration system – one that addresses the root causes of displacement and movement, and provides people with possible safe, authorised routes for journeying to a new place if they cannot remain at home. In the Bible, care and justice are seen to be two sides of the same coin, as the prophet Micah articulates:

> *He has told you, O mortal, what is good; and what does the Lord require of you but to do justice, and to love kindness, and to walk humbly with your God? (6.8)*

Given that many people would not migrate if it were possible to live a good life at home, there is an urgent need to address poverty (caused by struggling local economies and global economic inequality), political instability and violence, inadequate societal infrastructure, and climate change among other issues in countries of origin – all of which play varying roles in different contexts, and which tend to intersect complexly and exacerbate one another. As Alexander Betts and Paul Collier point out, refugee migration (and the same could be said for much other underprivileged migration too) is 'not only a humanitarian issue but also one of development ... It has to be about restoring people's autonomy through jobs and education'.[26] Betts and Collier see fragility – a fragile state being 'a poor country marked by weak state capacity and legitimacy' – as the main determining factor of displacement today.[27]

More challenging still, justice-creating care requires us to interrogate and acknowledge how our own interactions with the rest of the world – including our national decisions to sell arms, offer moral or material support to a particular leader/regime, or to engage in a war – intersect with local and regional dynamics to create fragility and bring people to European shores. While border/immigration policy and foreign, development/aid and trade policies are currently rarely, if ever, discussed together or presented in the media as linked, a more holistic policy approach is required.

Finally, justice-creating care is best offered in solidarity *with* migrants – standing alongside and working with those currently unsettled as allies – rather than a one-way paternalistic processing of giving to. We need to offer care as part of a mutual relationships that recognise that *we* are in this *together* – that many of our problems are ones we share in common and that solutions will therefore also be found together.[28]

While I have highlighted the persistent call for care, justice and solidarity to be practised with and among migrants, the Bible also invites us into the experience of those within established communities who have less positive views about offering hospitality to newcomers. Important questions have been raised in the past and today as to how the needs and rights of those outside a particular (national) community should be balanced with the needs and rights of those who belong to it. How can we engage in justice-creating care for new arrivals when we are struggling to find jobs, healthcare and educational opportunities ourselves?

What would it mean for our culture, identity and way of life – never mind security – if we were to allow in people who are different from us? What are the limits to our hospitality and who should we prioritise, given that we cannot provide for everyone?

Reflecting the reality that complex human beings have varied opinions and responses to these questions and the people they encounter, there are texts within the Hebrew Bible whose authors contest the prevalent calls for inclusion and care discussed above.[29] The books of Ezra and Nehemiah demand the expulsion of foreign wives and blame 'foreigners' for the conquest of Jerusalem and exile, and numerous verses express divine wrath for foreign nations and call for their annihilation (e.g. Exodus 23.23; Deuteronomy 2.34; Joshua 12; Isaiah 13; Esther 9.5; Genesis 9.18–27). Some of these texts were written at the same time as those advocating for inclusion and hospitality – though in later material, it seems the *ger* was not just to be treated justly but was to be included almost completely within the community.[30]

If we investigate the reasons for these more exclusive attitudes, fear of loss of culture, language, identity and religion; real and potential threats to security and autonomy; and internal and external wranglings over money, land and power, were all at play.[31] Early Christians too debated whether the salvation promised by Jesus was just for Jews or whether Gentiles could be included in God's promises too – with the Apostle Peter first seeing Christianity as only for Jews, and then having a dramatic conversion experience that led him to reach out to Gentiles (Acts 10).

The Bible does not offer a simple resolution to the questions of how many and who should be prioritised in terms of care, hospitality and justice – and just as political philosophers have continued to debate the pros and cons of communitarianism (prioritising those within the community, tending to lead to more closed borders) and cosmopolitanism (emphasising our common humanity and shared human rights, tending to lead to more open borders), so theologians have continued to grapple with what the calls for love of neighbour and love of stranger mean in our world today.

Some have argued more for universal rights and cosmopolitanism, while others have stressed the importance of national borders and identity.[32] We need to enter into conversation about how we can simultaneously cross borders to offer care to all human beings in need – including those far from us – *and* recognise that our families and communities – those near to us – deserve particular attention. As David Hollenbach writes, 'Christian love requires both *universal* respect for all and *distinctive* concern for those with whom we have special relationships.'[33] This involves attending to moral ideals as well as to what is practicable and likely to lead to individual and communal human flourishing in the light of contemporary social, political and economic realities and national, regional and international governance structures – a multi-faceted task that lies beyond the scope of this chapter.

What the Bible does do, however, is make clear that compassion for the most vulnerable – migrant and non-migrant alike – is a virtue to be cultivated and practicing justice-making care an ethical imperative. Calls for compassion, love of stranger, hospitality and justice are bells that resound again and again in the biblical tradition.

Blessing through encounter with the 'other'

A further insight that biblical reflection offers in relation to migration subverts the dichotomy presented in much debate today – the idea that either migrants or non-migrants/settled communities can thrive, but not both. The Bible, by contrast, suggests that we can receive blessing through encounter with those we see as 'other' – that we have a chance to meet God in and through those who seem new or strange to us. Engaging in hospitality with migrants can offer those of us who are not currently migrating an opportunity to grow, as much as it can offer possibility of new life to those seeking home in a new place.

Returning to the story of Abraham, Genesis 18 narrates how God appeared to him through three strangers who arrived at his tent and to whom he offered water to wash their feet and bread for their refreshment. These strangers gave him a message that Sarah, his wife, would have a longed-for son – a seemingly impossible dream given that she was past child-bearing age. This story gave rise to Hebrews 13.2, which recognises that in showing hospitality to strangers, 'some people have entertained angels without knowing it' – angels being bearers of God in the Bible, conduits of theophany or encounter with the divine.

The story of Ruth similarly suggests that migrants and newcomers can be bringers of new life. Ruth was a Moabite who travelled to Israel with her Israelite mother-in-law following the death of her husband and famine in Moab. As a widow without children, she would have carried shame, and Moab was considered the archenemy of Israel. It was associated with refusing to help Israelites on their way to the Promised Land and born from incest.[34] Yet, Ruth's presence and actions reinvigorate Israel, and bring new life to Naomi and to Boaz, a prominent figure in Bethlehem at the time. Ruth propositions and marries Boaz, and they have a son, Obed. Obed brings Boaz joy and fills Naomi's emptiness (4.13–17), and he becomes the grandfather of messianic King David, and is mentioned in the genealogy of Jesus (Matthew 1.5).

Ruth also encourages the community to interpret Torah law more generously, drawing them to see life that comes through inclusion of outsiders. Her name probably comes from the Hebrew root, *rwh*, meaning to water to saturation or to satisfy: it is Ruth who revives and re-enlivens a dry and struggling Israel – and who plays a key role in salvation history.[35] Or as Bergant has put it,

The story of Ruth demonstrates that openness to, and incorporation of, the vulnerable migrant is the way to restoration or salvation… the blessing of salvation comes from without (God) not from within (ourselves). [36]

The New Testament shares similar wisdom that it is the one who is different from us – the newcomer, the unknown, the stranger – who can bring new life. In Mark 7.24–30, Jesus encounters a Syrophoenician woman who, being a Gentile, was outside his community – likely culturally Greek and ethnically Syrian – and the encounter takes place in Tyre, a region usually seen negatively in the Hebrew Bible as greedily exploiting poorer Galilee. She is also a woman associated with a demon-possessed daughter, which would have been seen as polluting and marginalised her further. She comes to Jesus asking him to heal her daughter, but he refuses. She challenges him, and he changes his mind. This woman brings the word of God or *logos* (7.29) to Jesus, encouraging him to expand his message and ministry of salvation to Gentiles. So, just as Jesus heals her daughter – bringing both women the possibility of restoration – she also brings insight to him and hope to all looking for renewal.

In the Parable of the Sheep and the Goats, Jesus says 'Truly I tell you, just as you did it to one of the least of these who are members of my family, you did it to me' (Matthew 25.40), revealing that he – the divine – is present in those who are sick, hungry, in prison, naked and strange. Similarly, in the parable of the Good Samaritan (Luke 10.25–37), while insiders – established religious leaders, a priest and a Levite – ignore and walk past a man who has been robbed and injured, an outsider – a Samaritan – demonstrates compassion, kindness and mercy and is revealed to have done right. In telling this story, Jesus is blurring the boundaries between inside and outside, between the perceived centre and the edge, and suggests that God can be found in all and that the gospel is for everyone.

Theologians have echoed these biblical insights, and argued that engaging 'otherness' – encounter with those who are different – is an intrinsic and essential element in coming to know God and ourselves, and necessary for growing in wisdom and fullness of life.[37] The Trinity – the understanding of God as an internal relationship between Father, Son and Holy Spirit or Creator,

Redeemer and Sustainer – has dialogue between otherness and difference at its heart.

Those engaged in practicing and reflecting on Christian hospitality have repeatedly emphasised that the one who may at the outset appear to be simply the guest is in fact also a host, and has much to offer. Hospitality is a mutual practice, in which all involved bear the divine *and* encounter divine newness and to which all can contribute something of great value to the community if they are given the chance. As Thomas Ogleetree has put it, 'To offer hospitality to the stranger is to welcome something new, unfamiliar, and unknown into our life-world … The stranger does not simply challenge or subvert our assumed world of meaning; she may enrich, even transform, that world.'[38] In 1934, T.S. Eliot wrote a poem called 'Choruses from The Rock'. It contains this line, 'O my soul, be prepared for the coming of the Stranger. Be prepared for him who knows how to ask questions.' Strangers – whether immigrants, refugees, those settled if we are migrating, or others who are different from us – can ask us questions we never dreamed of; they can stretch our understanding and challenge our assumptions. They can inspire us to see ourselves and the world in an entirely new way. Strangers can offer us an encounter with the divine.

What does this mean in practice in relation to migration today? Aside from encouraging us to engage with migrants and to look for the gifts that they may bring into our communities – gifts that go significantly beyond the clichés of new cuisine and music, or skill sets that the NHS, scientific world or agricultural and other industries desperately need; and are perhaps more importantly about subtle and deep shifts in perspective and understanding – this challenges the assumption that responding to the needs and hopes of migrants and receiving communities is a zero-sum game. Much of our contemporary public, political rhetoric and policy around migration assumes that if migrants are welcomed, established communities will suffer; if migrants are working and their children go to schools and use the NHS, there will be insufficient job opportunities and resources for settled members of receiving societies.

If, however, we are blessed through encounter with 'others', it is possible that all can grow and be enriched through migration. This is not to say that there are not challenges and risks for both migrants and established communities in this encounter, or that this is easy. All too often, those already experiencing vulnerability are expected to support or make way for others experiencing vulnerability while those who are affluent and living in privileged security watch from the sidelines, untouched. This needs to be challenged, and calling for hospitality for migrants necessitates a simultaneous struggle for greater equality and fairness within our society – between people of different class, ethnic, age, gender and national backgrounds. What it is to say is that migration carries the potential for mutual blessing and enrichment, and that this invariably occurs through a messy and complex process that is enfleshed in local communities and real one-to-one encounters between human beings.

Conclusion: crossing borders

Where does biblical and theological reflection leave us in relation to contemporary migration? It leaves us with a call to cross borders and overcome barriers, as Daniel Groody has suggested.[39] The idea of the *imago dei* – that the image of God found in every human being, migrants and non-migrants alike – means we need to cross a border from seeing migrants as problems to seeing migrants as people.[40] Migration and home-seeking lie at the heart of what it means to be a human being, and all currently migrating therefore need to be treated with dignity and respect.

The concept of the *verbum dei* – the word of God – reminds us that God crossed the divine-human divide to live as Jesus, the living word, on earth.[41] If we are to take part in the *missio dei* – the mission of God in the world – we need to work to break down divisions that separate human beings from one another.[42]

This means reaching out to others with compassion and in solidarity, and working for just societies and fairer migration policies for all.

Finally, the *visio dei* – or vision of God – reminds us to raise our eyes to see over the boundary walls and barbed wire fences we have constructed around our nation states, and to revitalise our sense of connection with all people rather than just those within our particular nation.[43] We need to move from a fixation with country to a broader understanding of what the kindom of God might mean.[44] This is a kindom in which all have potential to bring and receive gifts, and to offer new life to one another. Such a vision holds up encounters between those who are different from one another as potentially enriching and God-bearing, and such a vision can energise us for the hard, messy, embodied work of building local and global communities together in which all can live and flourish.

ENDNOTES

1. Minh-ha, T.T. (2011) *Elsewhere, Within Here: Immigration, Refugeeism and the Boundary Event.* New York and London: Routledge.

2. Weil, S. (1949) *The Need for Roots.* Oxford: Routledge.

3. See for example Mavelli, L. and Wilson, E.K. (2017) *The Refugee Crisis and Religion: Secularism, Security and Hospitality in Question.* London: Rowman and Littlefield; Rose, A. (2012) *Showdown in the Sonoran Desert: Religion, Law and the Immigration Controversy.* Oxford: Oxford University Press; Saunders, J., Fiddian-Qasmiyeh, E. and Snyder, S. (2016) *Intersections of Religion and Migration: Issues at the Global Crossroads.* New York, NY: Palgrave.

4. For a discussion of how the Bible can inform debate, see Houston, F. (2015) *You Shall Love the Stranger as Yourself: The Bible, Refugees, and Asylum.* New York and Abingdon: Routledge; and Rogerson, J. (2007) *According to the Scriptures? The Challenge of Using the Bible in Social, Moral and Political Questions.* London: Equinox.

5. Gill, N. (2016) *Nothing Personal? Geographies of Governing and Activism in the British Asylum System.* Oxford: Wiley-Blackwell.

6. Said, E. (2001) *Reflections on Exile and Other Essays.* London: Granta Books.

7. Minh-ha, T.T. (2011) *Elsewhere, Within Here: Immigration, Refugeeism and the Boundary Event.* New York and London: Routledge.

8. Goodhart, D. (2017) *The Road to Somewhere: The Populist Revolt and the Future of Politics.* London: Hurst.

9. Bruggemann, W. (2001) *The Land: Place as Gift, Promise, and Challenges in Biblical Faith.* 2nd edition. Minneapolis: Augsburg.

10. Snyder, S., Kassam, Z. et al. (2013) 'Theologies and Ethics of Migration: Muslim and Christian Perspectives.' In Garnett, J. and Harris, A. *Rescripting Religion in the City: Migration and Religious Identity in the Modern Metropolis.* Farnham: Ashgate, p.21.

11. Jean-Pierre Ruiz offers fascinating readings of biblical texts from the perspective of migrants in Ruiz, J. (2011) *Readings from the Edges: The Bible and People on the Move.* Maryknoll, NY: Orbis.

12. Farisani, E. (2004) 'A Sociological Analysis of Israelites in Babylonian exile.' *Old Testament Essays* 17, 3.

13. Robert Carroll has described the Bible as 'the great metanarrative of deportation, exile and potenital return.' See Carroll, R. (1997) 'Deportation and Disaporic Discourses in the Prophetic Literature', in Scott, J.M., ed. (1997) *Exile: Old Testament, Jewish and Christian Conceptions.* Leiden: Brill, 64.

14. Moxnes, H. (2003) *Putting Jesus in His Place: A Radical Vision of Household and Kingdom.* Louisville: Westminster John Knox.

15. Barth, K. (2004) '*The Doctrine of Reconciliation*'. *Church Dogmatics, IV.1.* London: T&T Clark International, pp.157–210.

16. Quoted in Wogaman, J.P. and Strong, D. (1996) *Readings in Christian Ethics: A Historical Sourcebook.* Louisville: Westminster John Knox, 17.

17. Meeks, W. (2003) The First Urban Christians: *The Social World of the Apostle Paul.* 2nd edition. New Haven: Yale University Press.

18. Shafiq, M. (1998) 'Immigration Theology in Islam.' In Timani, H., Jorgenson, A. and Hwang, A. (2015) *Strangers in this World: Multireligious Reflections on Immigration.* Minneapolis: Fortress.

19. See Inge, J. (2003) *A Christian Theology of Place.* Aldershot: Ashgate, 37.

20. These terms and a discussion of their meanings can be found in Agamben, G. (1998) *Homo Sacer: Sovereign Power and Bare Life.* Stanford: Stanford University Press; Malkki, L. (1995) *Purity and Exile: Violence, Memory and National Cosmology among Hutu Refugees in Tanzania.* Chicago: University of Chicago Press; and Arendt, H. (1951) *The Origins of Totalitarianism.* San Diego, CA: Harcourt Brace Jovanovich.

21. Mountz, A. (2010) *Seeking Asylum: Human Smuggling and Bureaucracy at the Border.* Minneapolis: University of Minnesota Press, 155 and 162. For a discussion, see Snyder, S. (2015) 'Looking through the Bars: Immigration Detention and the Ethics of Mysticism.' *Journal of the Society of Christian Ethics,* 35, 1, 167–187.

22. See also Exodus 22.21; Jeremiah 22.3; Deuteronomy 10.17–19. Sacks, J. (2002) *The Dignity of Difference: How to Avoid the Clash of Civilizations*. London: Continuum, p.58.

23. Houston, F. (2015) *You Shall Love the Stranger as Yourself: The Bible, Refugees, and Asylum*. New York and Abingdon: Routledge.

24. Groody, D. (2009A) 'Jesus and the Undocumented Immigrant: A Spiritual Geography of a Crucified People.' *Theological Studies* 70, 2, 298–316.

25. Levinas, E. (1985) *Totality and Infinity: An Essay on Exteriority*. Pittsburgh: Duquesne University Press.

26. Betts, A. and Collier, P. (2017) *Refuge: Transforming a Broken Refugee System*. London: Penguin Allen Lane, p.10.

27. Ibid., p.18.

28. On solidarity, see Rieger, J. and Henkel-Rieger, R. (2016) *Unified We are a Force: How Faith and Labor Can Overcome America's Inequalities*. St Louis: Chalice Press and Sobrino, J. and Hernandez-Pico, J. (1985) *Theology of Christian Solidarity*. Maryknoll: Orbis.

29. Smith-Christopher, D. (1996) 'Between Ezra and Isaiah: Exclusion, Transformation, and Inclusion of the "Foreigner" in Post-Exilic Biblical Theology.' In Bret, M. (1996) *Ethnicity and the Bible*. New York: Brill, pp.117–142.

30. Van Houten, C. (1991) 'The Alien in Israelite Law.' *JSOT Supplement* Series 107. Sheffield: JSOT/Sheffield Academic Press, 175. It is important to recognise that different Hebrew words were used to designate different categories of stranger, and also that these meanings changed over time. For example, the nokrim and zarim were those completely outside Israel – real foreigners, who lived in the land/country beyond.

31. Snyder, S. (2012) *Asylum-Seeking, Migration and the Church*. Abingdon: Ashgate, on the reasons behind these views and practices in Ezra and Nehemiah, and also Southwood, K. (2012) *Ethnicity and the Mixed Marriage Crisis in Ezra 9-10: An Anthropological Approach*. Oxford: Oxford University Press. The term/category 'foreigners' in these books is complex.

32. See Heyer, K. (2012) *Kinship Across Borders: A Christian Ethic of Immigration*. Georgetown University Press, Bretherton, L. (2006) 'The Duty of Care to Refugees, Christian Cosmopolitanism, and the Hallowing of Bare Life' *Studies in Christian Ethics*, 19, 1, 39–61; and Biggar, N. (2015) *Between Kin and Cosmopolis: An Ethic of the Nation*. Cambridge: James Clarke for some varied points of view.

33. Augustine of Hippo and Thomas Aquinas both articulated that there were priorities in love. See Hollenbach, D. (2016) 'A Future Beyond Borders: Reimagining the Nation-State and the Church.' In Brazal, A. and Dávila, M.T. eds. *Living With(Out) Borders: Catholic Theological Ethics on the Migrations of Peoples*. Maryknoll: Orbis, pp.223–235, 228.

34. See La Cocque, A. (2004) Ruth: *A Continental Commentary*. Minneapolis: Augsburg Fortress, 3.

35. Ibid, p.40; Donaldson, L. (2010) 'The Sign of Orpah: Reading Ruth Through Native Eyes', in Pui-Lan, K. ed. (2010) *Hope Abundant: Third World and Indigenous Women's Theology*. Maryknoll, Orbis, pp.138–151, 146.

36. Bergant, D. 'Ruth: The Migrant Who Saved the People'. In Campese, G and Ciallella, P. eds., *Migration, Religious Experience, and Globalization* (2003) New York: Center for Migration Studies, pp.49–61, 60. For more in-depth discussion of Ruth and the story of the Syrophoenician Woman discussed below, see Snyder, S. (2012) *Asylum-Seeking, Migration and the Church*. Abingdon: Ashgate.

37. See for example Volf, M. (1996) *Exclusion and Embrace: A Theological Exploration of Identity, Otherness and Reconciliation*. Nashville: Farnham.

38. Ogletree, T. (1985) *Hospitality to the Stranger: Dimensions of Moral Understanding*. Philadelphia: Fortress Press, pp.2–3. See also Nouwen, H. (1976) *Reaching Out*. Glasgow: Collins, and Wells, S. (2006) *God's Companions: Reimagining Christian Ethics*. Oxford: Wiley-Blackwell, p.107.

39. Groody, D. (2009B). 'Crossing the Divide: Foundations of a Theology of Migration and Refugees', *Theological Studies*, 70.

40. Ibid.

41. Ibid.

42. Ibid.

43. Ibid.

44. Ada-Maria Isasi-Diaz proposed the concept of the kin-dom of God as a more inclusive, less patriarchal version of the kingdom of God in *En La Lucha: A Hispanic Women's Liberation Theology* Minneapolis: Fortress Press, 1993.

6

Cultural Identity in Post-Brexit Britain

A Thought on Narrative Healing

Mohammed Girma, London School of Theology and University of Pretoria

Brexit: from fear to fear

The formation of the European Union had two major objectives: to put an end to the bloody history of conflict between European nations, and to contain a potential threat from post-fascist Germany. This project stemmed from fear; but one could legitimately argue that it was a positive fear in that it aimed to maintain peace and tranquillity.

The first goal has been broadly achieved because the union has reached a stage in which it can speak into common issues with one voice, even though each new and emerging challenge provides it with a unique complexity to overcome.[1] Moreover, political developments in the twenty-first century seem to have erased any lingering fear that European nations would slide back into another world war.

The second goal might have already lost its relevance precisely because of the growing stability of democratic institutions and the advancement of more liberal way of life in Germany. Therefore, it is safe to say that, at the present stage, neither of the two rationales provide a sufficient ground for pushing European integration further.

There is, however, a third, and even more positive, rationale for the union: the economically integrated Europe is a path to growth and welfare. As a way of achieving this, in 1950, the European Coal and Steel Community begin to unite a number of countries economically and politically to secure lasting prosperity and peace.

Economic integration has gradually attracted more and more countries to the Union because it has proven to be a means of exchange by which people, goods, services and capital move at ease in the context of the single market and (with a few exceptions among specific members, including the UK prior to Brexit) the single currency. In fact, this was deemed a way of ensuring the social, economic and individual flourishing of citizens who share a 'European identity'. One of the practical outcomes of such a provision is that citizens can live and work anywhere within the Union with no need to fulfil legal requirements that other foreigners would do. In a *New York Times* article in 2012, Santiago Zobala, a continental philosopher at the University of Barcelona, points out that the formation of such an encompassing identity gave an impression that Europe had reached the end of history.[2] After decades of war and turmoil, it is as if the continent is united culturally, politically and economically. It even appears as if the Union is evolving towards adding a military element.

However, some social theorists have been warning that such an optimism could be short lived. Part of the reason is the lack of clarity, and ongoing concerns over the political and political-philosophical principles upon which the Union was founded. The philosophical puzzle of whether or not the relationship between the Member States will be based on monism, pluralism or dualism remains unresolved.[3]

There is no lack of philosophy of states in the continent; neither does it need to look abroad for social values such as liberty, equality, democracy and justice. However, the leaders have not reached a consensus as to whether or not traditional philosophies and values, often deployed to single states, should be applied to the Union. As Larry Siedentop pointed out, 'Europe is more than a confederation and less than a federation – an association of sovereign states which pool their sovereignty only in very restricted areas to varying degrees, an association which does not seek to have the coercive power to act directly on individuals in the fashion of nation states.'[4]

This constitutional and philosophical ambiguity, coupled with growing economic transnationalism and decreasing autonomy of the nation state, seems to have created palpable uneasiness in a significant portion of the British population. Studies indicate that social and economic changes brought by the Union are greeted with anxiety, especially, among the less educated and older demographics.[5] There seem to be two main factors behind the new fear. The first factor is the alienation of the working class. They feel disenchanted with the ruling class because of the breakdown of their narrative. Namely, workers find it very difficult to trust the story that the single market will provide them with the promised bright future.

The second factor is that the working class feel that their resources, their culture and identity are under threat because of the influx of cultural newcomers. EU-enforced assimilation into a new social model strikes them as threatening, because the new social and political order comes with a potential to alter the picture of Britain as they have known it. As a result, anti-immigration and anti-establishment sentiment dominated the argument in favour of Brexit. Between the two official referendum campaigns, 'Britain Stronger in Europe' and 'Vote Leave', the battle lines were the economy versus immigration. In other words, the British population was urged either to vote Remain to avoid the economic risks or vote Leave to regain control of borders and restrict immigration.[6] Both campaigns used fear as a political vehicle; but the fear of 'the other' triumphed over the fear of economic collapse.

Studies provide us with ample evidence that the fear of the negative impact of immigration on employment, wages and public services is unfounded.[7] However, the fear about cultural identity cannot be dismissed with a simple arithmetic analysis. The reason is that the question of identity is about who people take themselves to be as well as who they want others take them to be. Self-perception is built with a variety of elements including nationality, religion (or the absence of it), ethnicity, language, place of birth, political allegiances, certain values and norms, etc. People respond with anxiety and fear when they feel some of these designations are undergoing involuntary changes. A typical example is *The Strange Death of Europe* (2017) – a recent book by Douglas Murray, a British journalist and commentator. 'Europe', his book warns, 'is committing suicide.'[8] This is because, in his perception, European races, values and religions are under threat. As the 'world decides to migrate to Europe' while Europeans are losing their faith in themselves and their civilisation, Murray laments, these elements of identity are giving way to new ones. Places dominated by newcomers resemble their own origins – they eat their own food, speak their own languages and hold on to the religions of their origin. Therefore, according to Murray, British people are doomed to lose the only place in the world they have to call home.[9]

It is very simplistic, to say the least, to trivialise the expressions of anxiety offhand as mere scaremongering and xenophobia. The genuineness of the fear, and its impact on society, is beyond contention. Britain has become a deeply divided society. Fear is now a favourite tool often used by political entrepreneurs to win votes. Moreover, it is being socialised and made a part of culture and rhetoric. Walls and borders, in both the literal and metaphorical senses, have become a constant fixture in political vocabulary. As Ruth Wodak rightly pointed out, 'Body politics are therefore integrated with border politics.'[10] One of the hallmarks of the politics of fear is instrumentalising ethnic, linguistic or religious minorities as scapegoats and depicting them as inherent causes for current social woes. Cultural newcomers are painted as dangerous and threatening national identity.[11]

Let us say, for the sake of argument, that post-Brexit Britain would be able to effectively control its borders and reduce the number of newcomers. But, then, the world is already in the United Kingdom, to use Douglas Murray's mantra. The question, now, is: What is the best way to manage a society with plural identities? In what follows, after analysing multiculturalism – a very popular response implemented in the United Kingdom and some other European countries – I shall venture to make a case for as a better response to the challenges of cultural pluralism.

Multiculturalism: an answer?

Before examining how multiculturalism was played out in identity politics, it is important to briefly flesh out what it is. Multiculturalism is a concept with much-contested definitions. Tariq Modood writes that the meaning of multiculturalism changes depending on the country, institutional expression and local political culture.[12] However, let us look at the general characterisation put forward by Bhikhu Parekh, a British social theorist and one of the best-known architects of multiculturalism. In his *The Future of Multi-Ethnic Britain*, Parekh sees multiculturalism as a perspective on life which contains three central insights.[13] Firstly, multiculturalism assumes that human beings are culturally embedded and that as such they grow up in a culturally structured world. Culture helps them to organise their lives and social relations in accordance with its system of meaning and significance. Secondly, because of the limitations in a cultural system of meaning, multiculturalism fosters the realisation that different cultures grasp only a part of the totality of human existence. So the existence of 'other' cultures helps to enhance the understanding of oneself by expanding moral and intellectual horizons. Thirdly, multiculturalism assumes that all cultures, with the exception of the most 'primitive' ones, are plural in nature, needing continuous conversations between traditions and ways of thinking. Even though this does not mean there is no coherent root, it nevertheless stresses that cultural identity is inherently plural and fluid.

In their frequently quoted book *Changing Multiculturalism*, Joe Kincheloe and Shirley Steinberg identify diverse forms of multiculturalism.[14] Having regard to issues of relevance and the scope of the book, we will selectively discuss only a few of them. The first form is 'conservative multiculturalism' or 'mono-culturalism'. This form recognises cultural differences. However, it tends to believe in Western and patriarchal superiority, and as such sees migrants as culturally deprived. Life (including schools) is organised based on the perspective of white middle-class culture, where 'whiteness' is seen not as a particular form of ethnicity but as the most authentic and universal way of being.[15]

The second strand is the 'liberal form'. Its main focus is the individual. As a result, the liberal form stresses the natural equality of all individuals, regardless of race, gender and social class. This form sees lack of opportunity as the main cause of inequality. Moreover, it claims to adhere to ideological neutrality, in which some aspects of life should be free from politics. Ultimately, however, it subscribes to a conservative strategy of assimilation as a means of overcoming inequality between minorities and natives. The 'pluralist form', on the other hand, focuses on racial, class and gender differences, and aims to promote pride in group heritage. The main difference between pluralists and their liberal cousins is that while the liberals emphasise the individual, pluralists focus on groups.

Yet another form is identified by Kincheloe and Steinberg as 'critical multiculturalism'. Emanating from critical leftist ideology, it takes the issue of social class as its point of departure. In other words, this form requires people to understand the influence of dominant discourse on their racial self-image, political opinion and class.[16] The understanding of social class not only shapes consciousness, but also gives a parameter for social interaction precisely because, according to Kincheloe and Steinberg, it is a central organising principle. Even in schools, their pedagogical strategy aims to make learning a political process and help students to understand education as a struggle for social justice.[17]

Unlike the other forms outlined above, this form does not assume the uniformity of the human race, nor does it promote differences. Instead, Kincheloe and Steinberg claim that social injustice can be mitigated by both natives and migrants studying how race and class are politically, semiotically and educationally produced.

In this latter sense, multiculturalism is praised for being egalitarian, promoting equality and maintaining individual autonomy.[18] Furthermore, it is stated that multiculturalism was instrumental in providing a meaningful social narrative enabling people to fashion their lives on their own terms.[19] Some scholars see in multiculturalism something beyond the liberal chorus of individual autonomy. Namely, they broadly see it as a postcolonial way of understanding society, in which indigenous people are not dispossessed of their land and do not have their culture destroyed.[20]

Despite the constant attempts of reinterpretation by prominent scholars such as Parekh, Modood *et al.*, more recently multiculturalism has become a subject of severe scrutiny. One criticism of multiculturalism comes from scholars who see culture from a cosmopolitan viewpoint. Their argument is that we live in a time and a world that is full of movements and adaptations, in which one person can be a part of different cultures (and network identity). Consequently, critics think, it is implausible to develop cultural particularisms in the name of multiculturalism. We live in a world tied by technological and trade networks, overlapping economic interests, religious commitment and political imperialism and its offspring. By means of human mobility and mass migration we experience dispersion and cultural influences. In such a world, to immerse oneself in traditional practices involves an artificial dislocation from what actually is going on in the world.[21]

A second criticism of multiculturalism comes from those who think that liberal emphasis on individual rights would inevitably endanger group rights, especially the rights of vulnerable minority groups. For instance, according to Chandran Kukathas, multiculturalism might lead to a situation where governments passively watch 'communities which bring up children unschooled and illiterate; which enforce arranged marriages; which deny conventional medical care to their members (including children); and which inflict cruel and "unusual" punishment'.[22]

Yet again, others argue that multiculturalism is now outdated, and that, as a result, it is unable to bring about much-needed integration and cohesion in society. One scholar following this line of thinking is Jonathan Sacks, a prominent British intellectual and former Chief Rabbi. In his *The Home We Build Together* , Sacks announces that 'multiculturalism has run its course, and it is time to move on'.[23] Multiculturalism was a concept formulated to protect ethnic and religious minorities. Through a culturally sensitive process, one could argue, their identities have been affirmed, and the dignity of difference has been restored. However, Sacks qualifies, '…there has been a price to pay. [It] has led not to integration but to segregation'. Its original purpose was to promote tolerance; instead, according to Sacks, multiculturalism has made '…societies more abrasive, fractured and intolerant than they once were'.[24]

In their award-winning book *When Ways of Life Collide* (2007), Paul M. Sniderman and Louk Hagendoorn put forward an identical critique of multiculturalism in the Dutch social and political setting. Multiculturalism in the Netherlands, they point out, was intended to allow minorities to enjoy a better life and to win a respected place in their new society. However, their findings suggest that the outcome was the opposite – multiculturalism produced more exclusion rather than inclusion.[25] The reason, according to these scholars of Dutch minority studies, is that multiculturalism is like 'Joseph's coat' – it has many colours. When the colours strive to call attention to their differences, they undermine the unifying aspect of the 'coat'.[26]

While multiculturalism, in its variety of forms, has its own clear merits, its inability to bridge the understanding deficit is also equally glaring. For example, the conservative quest for the preservation of time-honoured practices and ways of life represents a legitimate concern. Externally forced deconstruction and redefinition of one group's world and social order – in this case, because of the cultural and religious newcomers in their territory – evokes fear and insecurity. However, the obsession with their own world causes them to turn a blind eye to the world of 'the other'. Instead of astutely negotiating change and continuity, they seek to maintain cultural hegemony at the expense of cultural minorities.

The liberal intention to protect the individual has its own unique merit precisely because, in some minority cultures, the individual's needs and rights are trumped in favour of a collective goal. Its weakness, however, comes from its strength – it tends to make society a collection of morally autonomous entities with no metaphysical and/or cultural glue to bring them together. As a result, cultural newcomers who are accustomed to a collective life system feel estranged in such an individualistic setting, and this, inevitably, is reflected in their educational performance.

One must also give due credit to the pluralist attempt to protect the position of vulnerable minority groups, because sometimes even democracy – however it is defined – can breed the tyranny of the majority. However, essentialist pride in group identity is a hindrance to seeing the nation (and wider society) as a forum of culturally, religiously and ideologically diverse individuals as well as groups. The critical multiculturalist intention to address the socioeconomic and political roots of social injustice by way of joint study also sounds a noble idea. However, it is not immediately clear how a joint forum is possible without recognising the organic unity of the human race. What is missing in multiculturalist discussion is a viable conceptual framework that brings about social cohesion in a culturally plural society. In what follows, I will attempt to develop a framework fitting for a Christian higher educational setting.

Narrative reasoning: a tool of healing

In the previous sections, I have endeavoured to show that the conflict of identities has created a threat to refreshed social harmony in a post-Brexit Britain. The climate of antagonism has been further reinforced by toxic political rhetoric during the campaign and surrounding terrorist attacks. A rise in xenophobic crime is symptomatic of a social malaise that has been brewing for some time. We have also seen that multiculturalism, instead of addressing the problem, has become a breeding ground for mutual suspicion. In what follows, I shall aim to offer *narrative reasoning* as an alternative solution.

But what is narrative reasoning? In the clinical domain, narrative reasoning is defined as a technique of affirming and/or transforming patients' identity by having clients tell their stories about the past and present, and by creating stories with them about the future.[27] Beyond strict interpretation of stories, narrative reasoning assumes human capacity, and as such, it takes biological anthropology as its point of departure. To wit, clinical practitioners claim that the human brain is wired in such a way to enable them to comprehend and put complex flow of actions into a coherent picture.[28] Narrative thinking, therefore, is a process by which humans understand and respond to social life around them. In narrative reasoning, the inner world of desire is examined and reconciled with the outer world of observable actions.

My argument shares some important tenets with the clinical domain. For example, it takes human capacity very seriously, in both biological and cognitive senses. In other words, the fact that the human brain is built in the same way shows that storytelling is a human activity that transcends time and culture.

However, my approach to narrative reasoning takes a different point of departure. First, it takes a cue from a Judeo-Christian thinking. In this vein, my characterisation goes beyond biological anthropology to seek metaphysical anchorage. Let me unpack this further. In the Judeo-Christian worldview, the material order came into being amid (creational) conversation. The scriptures tell us that the divine creational commands of 'Let there be…' gave birth to what we observe and experience. This indicates, both in literal and metaphorical senses, that storytelling is innate to the created order: God spoke, the creation responded. Furthermore, human persons have an additional quality of responding with a unique sense of purpose and responsibility. Among all life forms, only humans are endowed with an awareness of their finitude as well as the possibility of improvement. Their understanding of inherent finitude means they live with a sense of loss from which the moral duty of seeking the possibility of improvement springs.[29] The main tools of realising the possibility of self-improvement are creative freedom and living in and through discourse precisely because human persons are storytellers.[30]

Second, unlike the clinical version, the narrative reasoning I propose here is not based on a specialist–client relationship where one person is there to observe and guide another. It rather assumes the relationship between two equally important individuals, groups or communities who are willing to enter into each other's world by way of telling stories. And as such, instead of expecting transformation from one party, the fashion of storytelling here expects mutual transformation. Finally, narrative reasoning, here, does not require undoing one's identity in order to enter the conversation. Instead, it encourages maintaining a degree of positive self-perception without domineering the other party.

Now, let us imagine that different communities (with different stories shaping their identity) are willing to enter the conversation. The question is: What is the means of adjudication between the stories? I would suggest the adjudicator is 'the rationality of human heart'. One might argue that my assertion is now oscillating towards a Western orientation (which could be divisive in nature). That is, the political actors who take an anti-migration stance point out that they fear that migrants might come with religions and sets of values that threaten the Western way of life. Fair enough, culture changes to a degree, or is stretched to accommodate, when it entertains outsiders. But, we need to ask: What is the fundamental element that constitute the Western way of life? I would argue this is rationalism. Reason is what gave birth to Western civilisation. By demystifying the power of tradition and religious dogma, rationalism created the individual. This helped people to unleash their ingenuity and/or seek particular vocations as opposed to conforming to religious and cultural norms. Reason is the *a priori* principle that provides us with a reliable perception of the phenomenal world.[31] To fit into this Western culture, people are encouraged to create an environment that reinforces behaviours associated with such a style.

Non-Western migrants are not unfamiliar to with this concept of rationality. However, they see it through a synthetic relational prism more than as an abstract scientific point of reference. Their life system is fundamentally relational, and as such, the search for mechanisms to form abstract generalisations is not stimulated. From their standpoint, the distance between the observer and the observed is narrow. In fact, they see abstract rationalism as a divisive ideological commitment that excludes and marginalises ways of life that do not conform to it. Their understanding of reason is that it should be dialogical in nature. In dialogical rationalism, for one, the full picture is not sacrificed on the altar of scientific dissection, and for another, multiple aspects of being human – feelings, desire, aspiration and collective commitment – are fully accounted for.

To further clarify the role of reason in the multicultural setting, I highlight the distinction between the ontology of reason and its ideological manifestations. Ontologically, reason is an important, and even irreducible, aspect of human nature. It is an important way of being human and a universal system that helps humans to adjudicate between competing claims, and, eventually, to arrive at 'truth' – definable and acceptable belief.[32] In this sense, no society can stand without being subject to the power of reason. On this basis, one can legitimately argue that reason is not a Western invention; rather, it is something innate to human nature. Therefore, reason in this sense is ahistorical and transcultural – it has a binding force ensuing from the basic solidarity of people living together.[33]

True to this premise, cultural newcomers do not harbour any fear of rationality. However, they struggle to make a good sense of rationalism as an ideological commitment which elevates reason over other aspects of being human. Why is rationalism as an ideology a challenge for them? Rationalism as an ideology is a political project precisely because it serves as a means of excluding one to benefit the other.[34] This social exclusion happens when reason is used to universalise, one culture and way of life, and differentiate between what is culturally 'fit' and 'unfit'. In order to join the way of life with a universal endorsement narrative, one is supposed to undergo certain 'rites of initiation' such as bathing, as it were, in the water of the Enlightenment. This is because, according to Anibal Quijano, rationalism as an ideology embodies the colonial structure of power, producing discrimination at social, racial and economic levels.[35] Hence, making a distinction between the ontological and ideological natures of reason is an important step in circumventing cultural dominance in the mutual storytelling process.

This takes us to marrying reason to narrative to use it as a solution to the fear of 'the other'.

Argument against the exclusive dimension of rationalism and a call for narrative reasoning are not entirely the business of non-Western scholarship. It suffices to mention a few influential Western thinkers and schools who tried to highlight the ontological dimension of reason to mitigate the divisive outworking of rationalism. I shall, in what follows, briefly discuss G.W.F. Hegel[36] and Jürgen Habermas. For Hegel, reason is an instrument that heals social discord and that returns disintegrated life to its original form. This is because he sees reason as the 'substance of spirit' – the power that conquers the citadel of division by unifying the most tenacious of all oppositions.[37] For Hegel, the beauty of Jesus' life and teaching lies in his objective of 'restoring dismembered life into its original integrity'.[38] The instrument for such restoration of dismembered life is what he identifies as 'spirit', whose substance is reason. Christianity, according to Hegelian thinking, arose as the religion of spirit.[39] This is precisely because Christ is the ultimate storyteller in his deeds and words.

This has an important social implication. For Hegel, the kind of love and social commitment Jesus taught stems from a metaphysical origin, with an inner counterpart of beauty that heals social discord. In Hegelian understanding, love aims for the reconciliation of opposites and overcoming one-sided rationalism, one-sided emotionalism, or one-sided empiricism.[40] The power of spirit, according to Hegel, is not a positive power that isolates what is deemed to be 'negative'. Instead, it is the power that looks the negative in the face, and dwells with it in order to transform negative into positive. In this vein, Michael Hardimon seems right to brand Hegelian social philosophy as 'the project of reconciliation'.[41] True, Hegel did not have the influx of migrants in his mind; instead he was aiming to reconcile his contemporaries to the modern social order and overcome the sense of alienation from central institutions. However, despite differences in the (historical) contexts, overcoming alienation and social discord caused by rationalist 'lopsidedness' is an equally important challenge in culturally plural societies.

Habermas' understanding of reason has a crucial link to Hegel in that it stresses the importance of conversation and takes into consideration the asymmetry of power in the context of hegemony and dominance. In fact, Habermas himself characterised his philosophical project as 'reconciliation of a modernity which has fallen apart'.[42] 'In order to contribute to such reconciliation', Ronald Kuipers explains, 'his work seeks to address the high level of social fragmentation and alienation that modern societies exhibit, including the threats this situation poses to humanity's effort to achieve desperately needed social solidarity that is global in reach'.[43]

However, there is a stark methodological difference between them: while Hegel is thoroughly metaphysical in his approach, Habermas opts for a non-metaphysical approach. Even when he speaks of religion positively he maintains a stance of 'methodological atheism'. Notwithstanding his non-metaphysical stance, he concedes that reason is a modern evolution of the ancient Judeo-Christian notion of covenant.[44] However, he reveals in his rare autobiographical description that his understanding of reason and the public sphere was shaped by his personal experience, namely, a sense of alienation caused by illness and the two world wars. These experiences, he recounts, 'sharpened' his awareness of human interdependence. Highlighting the social nature of human beings, he explains that his understanding of reason is grounded on the hermeneutic tradition that emphasises the inter-subjective constitution of the human mind.[45] Habermas calls this the 'discursive model' of reasoning.

This model, according to Habermas, allows people of different races, classes and religious commitments to democratically channel their own formulations and conditions. The way he sees it, first, this model helps a person to be fully human by being accepted in the social world with open arms regardless of differences. Secondly, unlike the modernist rationalist approach – here he has John Rawls in mind – the discursive model is not constrained by conversational neutrality. Instead Habermas argues that conversation should be validated by 'practical discourse'. The framework that provides parameters for practical discourse, or normative constraint, is what he calls 'universal moral respect' and 'egalitarian reciprocity'.[46] Even though he tries to insulate his method from metaphysical conditions, it is clear that he could not entirely undo his metaphysical intuition.

Why is 'narrative reasoning' a more viable method to fill the hermeneutic deficit in a society that is in fear of diversity? First, it captures the internal logic of Judaeo-Christian ideas of community which gave birth to Western civilisation. In fact, tapping into a faint use of the metaphor of covenant, Sander Griffioen has expertly established the link between the Habermasian theory of communication and Christian understanding of the covenant. In this vein, Griffioen argues that while violence and betrayal can be associated with 'muteness' and 'speechlessness', covenant is expressed as an 'abiding force of communication'.[47] David Novak, a rabbinic scholar who is known for his political interpretation of the notion of covenant, argues that covenant is an interminable relationship of a historical community with its God, with its members as well as with outsiders.[48] This seemingly simple definition is laden with important assumptions worthy of a brief unravelling. For example, covenant assumes a plurality of identities. In fact, difference is the main prerequisite for covenanting. Parties come into covenant not despite their differences, but because of them. On this basis, informed by Christian ideals, the notion of dialectical inclusion is an important part of Western philosophical culture and can offer a foundation on which to start conversation.

Second, narrative reasoning fills the understanding deficit between cultural groups by giving agents ample opportunity to listen to each other. Listening assumes storytelling. True conversation, requires three elements: openness (as opposed to a defensive approach), accepting the genuineness and validity of others' point of view and empathy. To engage in conversation, therefore, is not an effort to objectively define the dialoguing partner from a neutral point of view; it rather is a process of mutual transformation. Far from one-sided objectification, such a journey of mutual transformation is a route to forming a common 'narrative identity'.[49] This can even be developed into collective and self-reflective inquiry that ventures to bring about social transformation.[50] The benefit of self-reflection is that it is not only directly linked to action, but it is also embedded in the understanding of history, culture and social relations.[51] In this vein, the introduction of non-European insights into the culture, and vice versa, could play a more humanising role for cultural new-comers as well as natives.

Finally, narrative reasoning helps migrants and natives to form a habit of positive social participation. Social participation on the other hand assumes, but also enhances, social cohesion. As Jonathan Chaplin rightly explains, social cohesion requires 'basic norms of sociality' such as trust, truthfulness and tolerance.[52] In Chaplin's view, the state cannot and should not take a lead in this process – even though the state might be involved in removing unjust obstacles. Rather, other institutions, such as churches, schools, families and neighbourhoods are better equipped to enhance social cohesion. The result of social cohesion is what Jonathan Sacks calls 'building a home together', based on the foundation of trust, truthfulness and tolerance. Multiculturalism has made us build not a 'home' but a 'hotel', where there is no sense of belonging and common purpose.[53] The participation in building a 'home' does not assume ahistorical and decontextualised individuals coming together and dialoguing about the shape of the home behind 'the veil of ignorance'. Instead, they come with their own historical contingencies, with their worldviews, primarily asking the question 'what is good for me?' In the meantime, however, they balance their cultural drive by asking the question 'what is good for my fellow humans?' This way the home becomes everybody's home, without trumping the cultural marks of individuals.

Conclusion

If I may indulge in an allegory, narrative – storytelling – is as close as the air we breathe, so much so that we do not often recognise it is around us. When the air we inhale is healthy, we utilise it without even being aware of its value. It becomes increasingly precious, however, as soon as we suffer the consequences of its pollution. Many parts of our world are suffering from narrative tragedy, and, unfortunately, Britain is not an exception. This is because the stories we are passing on have been contaminated by toxic political rhetoric, corporate greed, and, at times, sheer ignorance. The results are the fear of the other, the inability to see ourselves in others leading the society into mutual indifference, and, even worse, to violence. This endemic is prevalent not only between the people of different cultural orientations, but also between the ruling and working classes of the same culture.

Needless to say, there is no quick fix to this. Society, however, needs a starting point to move into a better future. This chapter, therefore, is a call for narrative healing. Multiculturalism, even in its heyday, could not bring narrative healing. Instead, it has crystallised the cultural compartments, making society unable to engage in meaningful conversation. Narrative reason with a Judeo-Christian root to it, therefore, enables people to come out of their cultural compartment to share their stories and listen to the story of the other in order to weave together one narrative identity.

ENDNOTES

1. Habermas, J. (2005) 'Why Europe needs a constitution.' in Eriksen, E.O., Fossum, J.E. and Menedez, A.J. eds. *Developing a Constitution for Europe.* Oxford: Routledge, p.7.

2. Zabala, S. (2017) 'How to be a European (Union) philosopher.' *The New York Times*, 23 February, 2017. Accessed 15 May 2017 at https://opinionator.blogs.nytimes.com/2012/02/23/how-to-be-a-european-union-philosopher

3. Dickson, J. and Eleftheriadis, P. (2012) *Philosophical Foundations of European Union Law.* Oxford: Oxford University Press, p.10.

4. Siedentop, L. (2000) *Democracy in Europe.* London, Penguin.

5. Becker, S.O., Fetzer, T. and Novy, D. (2017) 'Who voted for Brexit? A comprehensive district-level analysis.' CEP Discussion Paper No 1480.

6. Hobolt, S.B. (2016) 'The Brexit Vote: A Divided Nation, A Divided Continent.' *Journal of European Public Policy*, 23, 9.

7. Wadsworth, J. et al. (2016) 'Brexit and the Impact of Immigration on the UK.' CEP Brexit Analysis, 5.

8. Murray, D. (2017) *The Strange Death of Europe.* London: Bloomsbury.

9. Ibid., p.1.

10. Wodak, R. (1996) *The Politics of Fear: What Right-wing Populist Discourses Mean.* London: Sage.

11. Ibid., p.2.

12. Modood, T. (2005) *Multicultural Politics: Racism, Ethnicity and Muslims in Britain.* Edinburgh: Edinburgh University Press, p.4.

13. Parek, B. (2000) *The Future of Multi-Ethnic Britain: Report of the Commission on the Future of Multi-Ethnic Britain.* London: Profile Books.

14. Kincheloe, J.L. and Steinberg, S.R. (1997) *Changing Multiculturalism.* Buckingham: Open University Press, pp.3–5.

15. Jacobs, S. and Hai, N. (2002) 'Issues and Dilemmas.' In Anthias, F. and Lloyd, C. *Rethinking Anti-Racisms: From Theory to Practice.* London: Routledge.

16. Kincheloe, J.L. and Steinberg, S.R. (1997) *Changing Multiculturalism.* Buckingham: Open University Press, p.25.

17. Ibid., p.28.

18. Kymlicka, W. (2001) *Politics in the Vernacular: Nationalism, Multiculturalism, and Citizenship*. Oxford: Oxford University Press.

19. Appiah, A. (2005) *The Ethics of Identity*. Princeton: Princeton University Press.

20. Moore, M. (2005) 'Internal Minorities and Indigenous Self-Determination.' In Eisenberg, A and Spinner-Halev, J. (2005) *Minorities Within Minorities: Equality, Rights and Diversity*. Cambridge: Cambridge University Press.

21. Waldon, J. (1992) 'Minority Cultures and the Cosmopolitan Alternative.' *University of Michigan Journal of Law Reform*, 792–93.

22. Kukathas, C. (2003) *The Liberal Archipelago: A Theory of Diversity and Freedom*. Oxford: Oxford University Press, p.134.

23. Sacks, J. (2007) *The Home We Build Together: Recreating Society*. London: Continuum.

24. Ibid., p.3.

25. Sniderman, P.M. and Hagendoorn, L. (2007) *When Ways of Life Collide: Multiculturalism and Its Discontents in the Netherlands*. Princeton: Princeton University Press, p.5.

26. Ibid., p.5.

27. Boyt Schell, B.A. and Schell, J.W. eds. (2008) *Clinical and Professional Reasoning in Occupational Therapy*. Baltimore: Lippincott Williams & Wilkins, p.135.

28. Higgs, J. et al. (2008) *Clinical Reasoning in the Health Professions*. 3rd edition. Philadelphia: Elsevier Health Sciences.

29. Robert, H. (2011) *The Governance of Problems: Puzzling, Powering and Participation*. Bristol: Policy Press, p.7.

30. Niles, J.D. (2010) *Homo Narrans: The Poetics and Anthropology of Oral Literature*. Philadelphia: University of Pennsylvania Press, p.1.

31. Vajda, M. 'Reason and culture.' In Tymieniecka, A. (1993) *Reason, Life, Culture*. Gorinchem: Springer, pp.173–180.

32. Pole, D. (1972) 'The Concept of Reason.' In Dearden, R.F. *et al.* (1972) *Education and the Development of Reason*. London: Routledge, p.125.

33. Griffioen, S. (1991) 'The metaphor of the covenant in Habermas.' *Faith and Philosophy*, 8, 4, 528.

34. Race, R. (2011) *Multiculturalism and Education*. London: Continuum, p.54.

35. Quijano, A. (2007) 'Coloniality and modernity/rationality.' *Cultural Studies*. 21, 2–3, 168.

36. Note here that we are referring to later Hegel, rather than early Hegel, who tended to see more enchanting elements in Greek religions as opposed to Christianity.

37. Hegel, G.W.F. (2004) *The Philosophy of History*. Mineola, NY: Courier Dover Publications.

38. Kroner, R. (1971) 'Introduction to H.G.W. Hegel.' In Knox, T.M. *Early Theological Writings*. Chicago: University of Chicago Press, p.11.

39. Ibid., p.16.

40. Ibid., p.12.

41. Hardimon, M.O. (1994) *Hegel's Social Philosophy: The Project of Reconciliation*. Cambridge: Cambridge University Press, p.1.

42. Griffioen, S. (1991) 'The metaphor of the covenant in Habermas.' *Faith and Philosophy*, 8, 4, 125.

43. Kuipers, R. (2006) 'Reconciling Shattered Modernity.' In Boeve, L. *Faith in the Enlightenment? The Critique of the Enlightenment Revisited*. Amsterdam: Rodopi, pp.125–126.

44. For a more detailed discussion on this see Griffioen, S. (1991) 'The metaphor of the covenant in Habermas.' *Faith and Philosophy*, 8, 4, 125, 524–40.

45. Habermas, J. (1992) *Themes in Postmetaphysical Thinking: Philosophical Essays*. Cambridge, MA: MIT Press, p.14.

46. Benhabib, S. (1992) *Situating the Self: Gender, Community, and Postmodernism in Contemporary Ethics*. London: Routledge, p.105.

47. Griffioen, S. (1991) 'The metaphor of the covenant in Habermas.' *Faith and Philosophy*, 8, 4, 523.

48. Novak, D. (2005) 'The Covenant In Rabbinic Thought.' In Bergant, D. et al. (2005) *Two Faiths, One Covenant? Jewish and Christian Identity in the Presence of the Other*. Oxford: Rowman & Littlefield, p.72.

49. Flanagan, R. et al. (2007) 'TEMAS: A Multicultural Test and Its Place in an Assessment Battery.' *Handbook of Multicultural Assessment: Clinical, Psychological, and Educational Applications*. London: Wiley Publishers, p.323.

50. Freire, P. (1970) *Pedagogy of the Oppressed*. New York: Continuum.

51. Baum, F., MacDougall, C. and Smith, D. (2006). 'Participatory Action Research'. *Journal of Epidemiology and Community Health*, 60, 10, 854.

52. Chaplin, J. (2008) 'Beyond Multiculturalism – But To Where? Public Justice and Cultural Diversity.' *Philosophia Reformata* 73, 2, 204, 204.

53. Sacks, J. (2007) *The Home We Build Together: Recreating Society*. London: Continuum, 14.

7

Child Migration to the UK

Hopes and Realities

Pia Jolliffe and Samuel Burke OP

The authors thank Fr Richard Finn, OP, for his encouragement to write this chapter. We also thank Lord Hylton, Lord Dubs, Lord Alton, Dr Alice Freeman, Liz Teresa Slater and Gulwali Passarlay for discussing child migration to the UK with us.

In his messages for World Migrant Days 2017 and 2018, Pope Francis highlights the vulnerability of migrant children around the world. Over the course of several decades, the UK has been a popular destination for children seeking refuge from political violence. Historically, the saved thousands of children from the Nazi regime. Today, Section 67 of the Immigration Act 2016 (the 'Dubs amendment') calls for the similar welcome of young people who arrived in Europe in search for protection from conflict and violence in their own countries of origin but also from insecurity in refugee camps such as Calais. Based on interviews with politicians, aid workers and volunteers, this chapter draws attention to child migrants' vulnerability and assesses the impact of the Amendment 115 to Section 67 of the Immigration Act 2016.

Introduction

'I was 12 when my mother paid people smugglers $8,000 to take my brother and me from Afghanistan to Europe. After my father and grandfather were killed by US armed forces the Taliban put pressure on us to become suicide bombers. Drastic as it was, sending us away was the only option my mother could see to keep us alive. I then began a 12-month odyssey across Europe. I was separated from my brother almost immediately and incarcerated three times. I jumped from a speeding train in Bulgaria, nearly breaking both my legs, and almost drowned in a tiny overcrowded boat off the coast of Greece. When I arrived in the UK, I was still only 13, but almost unrecognisable from the child I had been. That's what hunger, cruelty and brutality does to you.'[1]

In his book Gulwali Passaray describes the painful process of age-assessment upon his arrival in the UK. Although he was only 13 years old, Kent Social Services concluded that he was 16 and a half years of age because of his mature appearance and clever answers to their interview questions. As a result of the incorrect birth date he had been given, he was only given discretionary leave to remain in the UK for one year. At the perceived age of 17 he was expected to leave the country or to be deported. Because the Home Office insisted on him being 16 years old, he had to share accommodation with adults instead of with children. Unable to accept this injustice, Gulwali made every effort to prove his real age and eventually – with the help of the educational institution Starting Point – managed to have his age re-assessed and his real birthday recognised.[2]

In conversation with Pia Jolliffe, Gulwali reiterates that the age-assessment has huge consequences for child migrants' lives. Those who are considered above 18 years are deprived of all sorts of opportunities like education and foster families. They are either kept in detention, deported or decide to go underground.[3]

Gulwali Passaray's story is shared by thousands of children and young people who arrive as unaccompanied minors in Europe. Indeed, in 2016, there were 63,300 unaccompanied minors among asylum seekers registered in the European Union. The majority of these minors were boys (89 per cent) and over two-thirds were 16 or 17 years old. The highest number of asylum applications by unaccompanied minors was registered in Germany (36,000, or 57 per cent of the EU total) followed by Italy (6,000, or 10 per cent), Austria (3,900, or 6 per cent) and the United Kingdom (3, 200, or 5 per cent). Over half of these unaccompanied minors said they were originally from Afghanistan (38 per cent) or Syria (19 per cent).[4] Like Gulwali Passarlay, these young people are highly vulnerable because of the hardships most of them suffered in their countries of origin, on their way to Europe and within the EU. What is particularly striking is the gender gap. Although many girls start going on journeys to Europe, they often disappear on their way. A social worker in a home for unaccompanied refugees in Austria mentioned in an interview with Pia Jolliffe that the boys in her care confirmed that there are many girls who disappear on their way to Europe: 'A bus stops, they enter the bus and then they are away. This gives me goose pimples.'[5]

Once the young people have arrived in Europe, they are not spared the humiliation that frequently comes with police interrogations. Often, the child's age is put into question supposedly because those under 16 receive a different treatment in foster arrangements than those older than 16. Gulawali Passaray described his experience as follows:

After being arrested and sent to an immigration centre I had my age assessment. They asked me questions about my family background, my journey – even silly questions about the province I came from in Afghanistan. After three or four hours they announced I was not 13 but 16-and-a-half. They said I couldn't have travelled so far when I was still so young, and that I was too smart to be 13. I know I looked older than I was – I still do, but I grew up in a harsh, mountain environment and had been through a long, hard journey. They tried to give me a new date of birth. I was so angry. I felt they were worse than the smugglers

– they had been heartless, but they hadn't tried to change my identity. I was so angry I ripped up the paper the assessors gave me, in front of them. (…) I didn't know why they were saying all this. Now I know it is because the Home Office have to put you in school and in foster care and give you the legal rights of a child if you are under 16.[6]

Clearly, migrants under the age of 18, especially girls, are vulnerable and face hazards related both to their gender and their age.

Pope Francis and the Church's teaching on migration

Pope Francis has a profound concern for migrants and refugees. In his message for World Migrant Day 2018,[7] the Holy Father said that his visit to Lampedusa on 8 July 2013 was a key moment in his engagement for the plight of those forced to flee their home countries.

In his previous message for World Migrant Day 2017,[8] Pope Francis highlighted the vulnerability of migrant children around the world. He emphasised that child migrants are threefold defenceless: first, because they are children, second, because they are foreigners and third because they have no means to protect themselves. The Holy Father then suggested three ways to respond to the reality of child migrants and refugees. Above all, he encouraged us to understand migration as part of salvation history.

Pope Francis exhorted us to work for the integration of children and young people. At the same time, he stressed the need to address the root causes of children's migration. In his message for World Migrant Day 2018, the Holy Father pointed to the *International Convention on the Rights of the Child* as a legal basis for the protection of child migrants. He emphasised that underage migrants must not be detained, but be cared for in temporary custody or foster programmes. Also, they need to have regular access to primary and secondary education. Moreover, the Holy Father emphasised the need to provide education opportunities for young people after their transition to legal adulthood.[9]

Pope Francis' messages for the 2017 and 2018 World Migrant days build upon the Catholic Church's long tradition of supporting migrants and refugees. Pope Pius XII's 1952 Apostolic Constitution *Exsul Familia*[10] is regarded as a key document in the Church Social Teaching on migration. The document opens with a reminder of how the Holy Family – Jesus, Mary and Joseph – had to flee to Egypt. The experience of forced migration is thus a very concrete way to follow in Christ's sufferings. The first part of the constitution then recalls the Church's care for migrants starting with St Ambrose through the centuries up to the teaching of Pope Leo XIII, who not only cared tremendously for the dignity and rights of wage labourers, but also for economic migrants who emigrated abroad.

In this respect, *Exsul Familia* also stressed the work of St Frances Xavier Cabrini who – inspired by Pope Leo XIII – went to North America to set up missionary schools for Italian emigrant children. The document also recalls several armed conflicts of the twentieth century and stresses how the Church cared for those who left their countries due to antireligious persecution. The second part of the constitution is dedicated to norms for the spiritual care of migrants. This section first recalls and modifies the enactments of previous Popes. This is followed by a description of the Office of Delegate for Migration Affairs whose function it is 'to foster and promote by every apt means the welfare, especially spiritual, of Catholic migrants of whatever language, race, nationality or, with necessary exception, rite'.

Another issue discussed is the role of missionaries to emigrants and ship chaplains as well as the spiritual care local ordinaries are to provide for foreigners. A special section focuses on Italian migrants who – at the time of writing of *Exsul Familia* – were the largest European emigrant group.

As the teaching of the Church evolved, the Church recognised the complexity of migration experiences. In 1969 Paul VI issued the Apostolic Letter in the Form of Motu Proprio *De pastorali migratorum cura*[11](On the pastoral care for migrants).

In this document, the Pontiff highlighted new forms of migration and stressed the need for pastoral care to pay attention to migrants' cultural, religious and linguistic backgrounds. At the same time, Paul VI stressed that these different social backgrounds need not be a cause of division. Instead, they need to contribute to peace and unity among the human family, quoting Scripture: (For in one Spirit we were all baptised into one body whether Jews or Gentiles, whether slaves or free, 1 Corinthians 12, 13–14); (For you are all one in Christ, Gal. 3.28).

On 19 March 1970, Pope Paul VI established the Pontificia Commissio de Spirituali Migratorum atque Itinerantium Cura (Pontifical Council for the Pastoral Care of Migrants and Itinerant People). The objectives of this Council are studying and providing pastoral care to 'people on the move' including migrants, refugees, fishermen, seafarers, air travellers, road transport workers, nomads, circus people, fairground workers, pilgrims and tourists, as well as other people who, for various reasons, migrate for education and work. Between 1999 and 2010, the Pontifical Council for the Pastoral Care of Migrants and Itinerant People published the journal *People on the Move*. In 2004, Cardinal Stephen Fumio Hamao wrote the Council's Instruction *Erga Migrantes Caritas Christi* (The love of Christ towards migrants). In this document, Cardinal Hamao emphasised the migrant as a gift and resource. Meditating the Church at Pentecost he noted:

> *Migrants' journeying can thus become a living sign of an eternal vocation, a constant stimulus to that hope which points to a future beyond this present world, inspiring the transformation of the world in love and eschatological victory. The peculiarities of migrants is an appeal for us to live again the fraternity of Pentecost, when differences are harmonised by the Spirit and charity becomes authentic in accepting one another.* [12]

Erga Migrantes Caritas Christi also speaks about the need of inculturation and interreligious dialogue. At the same time,

Cardinal Humao pointed out the particular plight of children caught up in trafficking. Children are also mentioned in regard to Catholic education for migrant children and in relation to family issues. There is, however, no special Church document on child migration until Pope Francis' letter.

History of the UK approach to child migration

The UK does not come to issue of child migration with clean hands but via a long and chequered history. For example, the UK's colonial history and its role in the transatlantic slave-trade provide some important historical perspective to the present debate. According to David Richardson, Professor of Economic History at Hull University and Director of the Wilberforce Institute for the Study of Slavery and Emancipation, approximately 3.4 million slaves were transported by British ships across the Atlantic; many of these were children.[13]

More recently, between the 1920s and 1967, the British government's emigration programme oversaw the expatriation of more than 130,000 vulnerable children between the ages of 3 and 14 to Canada and Australia. Some of the children sent were in the care of the government, others were in the custody of churches or charitable organisations, such as Barnados.

We might suppose the government had at least two good intentions in implementing the policy: first, they sought to relieve the burden on UK orphanages; and, second, they aimed to increase the populations of the colonies. Single mothers were told that their children were being sent to a new start in life. In reality, some of the children were destined for servitude at foster homes and state-run institutions where some were subjected to physical and sexual abuse at the hands of those charged with protecting them. This horrific abuse is now well-documented, having been uncovered in a series of investigations and disclosures through the tireless work of social worker, Margaret Humphreys, and the broadcaster, David Hill, himself a child migrant sent to Australia.

The British government subsequently recognised their role in the abuse and issued an official apology. In a statement in the House of Commons in 2010, the then Prime Minister Gordon Brown said, 'To all those former child migrants and their families... we are truly sorry. They were let down.' He added, 'We are sorry they were allowed to be sent away at the time when they were most vulnerable. We are sorry that instead of caring for them, this country turned its back.'[14]

This welcome apology for previous government complicity in the transportation of children and the sufferings they subsequently endured does not consign the maltreatment of unaccompanied migrant children to the history books. The numbers of unaccompanied child migrants coming to the UK have risen drastically due to armed conflicts and political instability in diverse places such as Afghanistan, Albania, Syria and Sudan. In 2012, around 1,200 unaccompanied migrant children sought asylum in the United Kingdom – about 5 per cent of the nearly 22,000 applications lodged in that year.[15] However, by 2016, the number of unaccompanied children applying for asylum had increased to 3290, about 16 per cent of all asylum applications.[16] As a result of this marked rise in children seeking asylum, the legal framework that processes these applications has been the subject of increased scrutiny.

The present law

In asylum cases concerning 'unaccompanied asylum-seeking children' (UASC) special legal provisions apply. Such children are entitled to protection under domestic legislation as well as international instruments, including the UN Convention on the Rights of the Child (UNCRC),[17] the European Convention on Human Rights and the 1951 UN Convention relating to the Status of Refugees and the accompanying 1967 Protocol.

Although not directly incorporated into UK statute law, the principles of the UNCRC guide domestic law and practice, and are often cited by the courts when interpreting obligations imposed by human rights and other legislation. At the core of the UNCRC is the paramount importance of the best interests of children. Article 3 of the Convention requires that 'in all actions concerning children and young people, whether taken by public or private social welfare institutions, courts of law, administrative authorities or legislative bodies, the best interests of the child shall be a primary consideration'. Furthermore, Article 22 of the United Nations Convention on the Rights of the Child (UNCRC) requires State Parties to take measures to ensure that children seeking asylum receive appropriate protection and humanitarian assistance in the enjoyment of the rights that the Convention provides.

In November 2008, the British government removed a reservation which allowed it not to apply the Convention in decisions concerning children and young people subject to immigration control. Subsequent to that, all children – irrespective of their immigration status – enjoy the rights and protections of the UNCRC as specified under Article 2 of the Convention.

This paved the way for the new domestic legislation requiring the Secretary of State to make arrangements to ensure that UK Border Agency (UKBA) functions are carried out having regard to the need to safeguard and promote the welfare of all children in the UK. Section 55 of the Borders Citizenship and Immigration Act 2009 places a duty upon the Secretary of State and the immigration authorities to discharge immigration functions, while having regard to:

> ...the need to safeguard and promote the welfare of children who are in the United Kingdom.

This wording reflects an almost identical duty contained within section 11 of the Children Act 2004, under which government agencies – such as the police and local authorities – are required to safeguard and promote the welfare of children. However, section 55 expressly limits this duty to those already in the country so, for example, the duty does not apply to immigration officials processing applications overseas.

When considering the legal framework of the UK, it should also be noted that while immigration policy is a reserved matter, responsibility for the care and support of unaccompanied children rests with the devolved administrations (i.e. the Scottish, Welsh and Northern Irish governments).

The courts have strived to underscore the primacy of the best-interest provision in section 55. In ZH (Tanzania) v Secretary of State for the Home Department,[18] Lord Kerr remarked that a child's best interest 'is not merely one consideration that weighs in the balance alongside other competing factors. Where the best interests of the child clearly favour a certain course, that course should be followed unless countervailing reasons of considerable force displace them [...] the primacy of this consideration needs to be made clear in emphatic terms.'[19]

Under EU Law, any unaccompanied minor with family in the UK has the legal right to be reunited under the terms of the Dublin III Regulations. The regulations prioritise respect for family unity over certain other considerations, such as which country the asylum seeker originally entered. However, this provision carries the practical difficulty of a child locating and contacting the relations in the UK from a remote location. The Red Cross has complained that EU Member States have not implemented the regulation 'proactively', leaving unaccompanied children to navigate complex asylum and legal systems themselves, often without support, in order to access their rights under Dublin.[20] As a means of ameliorating this difficulty, the British government has seconded officials to France, Italy and Greece to assist in the identification of qualifying cases under Dublin III. This will be financed from a £10 million DFID fund which will be used in part to identify children in Europe in need of family reunion in the UK.[21]

Many asylum applications, by their nature, are difficult to process. Given the extra legal protection afforded to children, the question of age is frequently at issue. Where there are grounds for doubt, and especially where documentation is not available, immigration caseworkers may dispute the age given by a child migrant, giving rise to possible age assessment litigation. In the case of R. (on the application of B) v Merton LBC [2003] EWHC 1689 (Admin); [2003] 4 All E.R. 280, the courts laid down so-called 'Merton guidelines' which outline the approach to be taken when conducting an age assessment. The Merton judgment was subsequently approved in R. (on the application of Z) v Croydon LBC [2011] EWCA Civ 59; [2011] P.T.S.R. 748.

Against this legal backdrop, Lord Dubs, a Labour Peer with an especially appropriate personal background, entered the fray.

Dubs Amendment

Lord Dubs was born in 1933 in Prague. His father was Czech and Jewish and his mother came from Austria. In an interview[22] with Pia Jolliffe, Lord Dubs stresses that although his father was not political at all, he sensed the danger of the Nazi regime and came in 1939 to England. His mother did not get permission to leave, yet she managed to put their son Alf on the Kindertransport to London. The Kindertransport was organised by Sir Nicholas Winton, who also arranged for foster parents to welcome the 669 children who travelled on Alf Dubs' train.

At that time Alf Dubs was six years old and one of the youngest children on board of the train. He remembers that it took 24 hours to reach the Dutch border: 'we just sat there and waited and when we got to the Dutch border, the older ones cheered, because we were out of reach of the Nazis. I didn't know what that meant, I just knew it was significant, but I didn't know why'. When being asked whether he remembers being afraid by it all, he said: 'I don't know. I don't know whether a six-year-old remembers being afraid or not. My mother put some little sandwiches in a backpack, and I hadn't eaten anything in the journey (…) so perhaps I was a bit upset by it all.'

Lord Dubs remembered how fortunate he was to have his father waiting for him at London Liverpool Street station, when most of the other children had no relatives in England and were instead welcomed by foster families. Eventually, his mother also succeeded in getting out of Prague and arrived on 31st August 1939 in London. This was also the day the war started and – Dubs emphasises – would she have been a day later, she would not have managed it.

In the 1930s, Britain was the only nation in the world to assist Jewish children in this way. At the time of our interview there were, according to Lord Dubs, 80,000–90,000 unaccompanied refugee children in Europe. Many of these children were in danger of being taken into prostitution, being subject to violence, being trafficked and so on. According to Lord Dubs (interview), young migrants were often ignorant about their rights. When he talked to Eritrean and Afghan refugees in Calais, they said that there was no official information about their rights on French territory. According to Italian authorities, across Europe 10,000 young people had disappeared altogether. Under the existing Dublin III scheme, migrant children with family in Europe were allowed to join their relatives. However, Dublin III did not provide for children without family in Europe. Lord Dubs was particularly struck by the situation of children and young people in the Calais camp, in France, but also by the situation of young people in countries like Italy and Greece. So, Amendment 115 to Section 67 of the Immigration Act 2016 (the 'Dubs Amendment') was introduced for the protection of boys and girls who had no family members in Europe.

Lord Dubs' amendment was originally intended to create a legal route for 3,000 child asylum seekers to enter the UK and have their claims considered. The final draft of the amendment removed the number 3,000 replacing it with the words 'a specified number'. However, the figure of 3,000 continued to be widely cited as the goal, with the final figure to be announced following discussions with local authorities. In May 2016, the government agreed to the amendment.

Subsequent to the passing of the 2016 Act including the Dubs Amendment, the Calais jungle was demolished but child migrants nevertheless continued to arrive in northern France.

The Dubs Amendment came into force on 31 May 2016. Six months later, on 27 October 2016, the Camp in Calais was demolished. After the closure of the camp around 700 child migrants were thought to apply for asylum in Britain. Forty per cent of these children said they had relatives in the United Kingdom. Those without relatives in Europe hoped to be granted asylum through the Dubs Amendment.[23]

However, on 8 February 2017, the Minister of State for Immigration announced in a written statement[24] that the 'Dubs' amendment would take around 150 more children from Europe (350 in total), far fewer than had been expected when the amendment to the bill was proposed. The minister also announced the completion of the Home Office Calais Procedure and the closure of the fast-track family reunification process. This leaves lone children in Europe to seek asylum in the European country in which they are present before waiting for their application to be processed, which can take as long as a year or more. Given that such children lack access to legal knowledge or services needed to make such a request, the route to reunification is effectively closed.

Commenting on the announcement, a spokesman for Downing Street cited the limitation of resources, saying that the scheme was 'dependent on the resources that councils can provide and the feedback that we have received is that we can deal with 350 children. There is a limit on the capacity local authorities have to provide that level of care'.[25]

The government's announcement prompted a substantial backlash. On 11 February, Lord Dubs delivered a petition in front of Prime Minister Theresa May's home at 10 Downing Street. The petition was signed by around 50,000 people.[26] Then Liberal Democrat leader Tim Farron denounced it as a 'betrayal of British values'.[27] Lord Dubs described the decision as 'shameful' and further questioned the manner of the announcement, commenting, '[i]t's been sandwiched between [Prime Minister's Questions] and all these votes on Brexit – what a way of hiding an announcement'.[28] Whereas the Red Cross stated: 'People traffickers thrive in the absence of safe and legal routes to protection ... we need to make sure that children are not left to fend for themselves in places such as the jungle camp again.'[29]

What has happened since then?

Moreover, members of the House of Commons criticised this small number and the NGO challenged the consultation on which the 350 number was based. The NGO's legal team was concerned about the surprising absence of any offers from the entire English south-west. Eventually, the Home Office conceded that it had 'missed' 130 places offered by local authorities in the English south-west. Therefore, the number of children to be relocated under the Dubs Amendment was raised to 480 on 26 April 2017. At that time, British newspapers started again reporting about migrants returning to flattened area of the previous camp. According to *The Guardian*, 'several hundred' people arrived and half of them were teenagers between 15 and 17 years of age. The local police tried to set up shelters for these unaccompanied minors but still found children at night on the streets.[30]

In spite of children and young peoples' ongoing presence at Calais, the government's position has not changed. In June 2017 the British NGO Help Refugees criticised the Home Office for their alleged failure to properly assess local councils' capacity to take in unaccompanied minors under Amendment 115 to Section 67 of the Immigration Act 2016 and took their case to the High Court. By the end of August 2017, Lord Dubs saw himself advocating against the government's decision to close the scheme.[31]

Looking forward

The Dubs scheme offered children and young people a safe way to arrive in the United Kingdom. Rather than exposing these young people to threats and hazards related to informal forms of border crossing,[32] the Dubs Amendment offered a transparent route and a welcome in the United Kingdom.

Other countries have taken a different tack. Italy is the first European country to give comprehensive protection to lone child migrants under the so-called 'Zampa law', passed in March 2017. The law sets minimum standards of care, limiting the time children can be kept in migrant reception centres. Local authorities have a ten-day window to confirm the identities. Furthermore, local authorities are prohibited from refusing unaccompanied and separated children at the border or if it could cause harm. That Italy has made such a move while overwhelmed with migrants is commendable. Save the Children estimates that more than 25,800 unaccompanied minors arrived in Italy by sea in 2016, more than twice as many as 2015.[33] In March 2017, it was reported that more than 3,000 unaccompanied minors arrived in the UK in 2016.[34]

In addition, Lord Alton has advocated using our Foreign Embassies as places where child migrants might register their interest in family reunification.[35] Such a measure would represent a more active effort on the part of the government rather than a rather passive approach, which given its remote location appears at best complacent, at worst irresponsible. Setting aside consideration of additional legal measures such as the Zampa law, the UK government could be far more creative in providing routes to settlement for those who might qualify under existing arrangements under measures such as utilising our Embassies as Lord Alton suggests.

Future risks

In an article in *The House* magazine, Lord Dubs envisaged political leadership that is able to draw a distinction between refugees and immigrants. Rather than saying 'the numbers are too high, let's keep the numbers down', Lord Dubs envisaged political leaders who can explain the government's position on refugees and various groups of migrants such as those arriving from EU countries and those arriving from other parts of the world for family reunion.[36]

Lord Dubs' concern is echoed by academics such as Paul Collier who called the conflation of refugees with migrants a key confusion.[37]

At the same time, it is – as highlighted by Pope Francis in his message for World Migrant Day – important to seek and adopt long-term solutions and to engage with the root causes of child migration. This point is endorsed by recent research that stresses the importance of developing approaches that make it unnecessary for parents threatened by war and poverty to send their children to Europe.[38]

During the writing of this chapter, Pope Francis issued a 20-point action plan on migrations to try and galvanise the international community on one of the most significant global challenges. In doing so, Pope Francis is helping to lay the groundwork for the UN Global Compacts to be adopted by the UN General Assembly in September 2018. At the heart of the 20 action points are four calls to action: to welcome, to protect, to promote and to integrate with the 'ultimate goal [of] building of an inclusive and sustainable common home for all'. The document puts the cause of migration into some important context. On the one hand, the Pope draws attention to the urgency of the issue, recalling 'the massive numbers of people who have been forced to leave their homes due to persecution, violence, natural disasters and the scourge of poverty'. But notwithstanding recent trends, the Pope also observes that the issue is perennial and should 'be recognised...as a natural human response to crisis and a testament to the innate desire of every human being for happiness and a better life'.[39]

More controversially, the Pope enjoined states to prioritise the personal safety and dignity of migrants over national security. It remains to be seen whether this reversal of traditional concerns will take place and what practical application it will have.

Within this general framework, children surely have a privileged place as the most vulnerable category of persons. As the Pope observed in 2017, 'among migrants, children constitute the most vulnerable group, because as they face the life ahead of them, they are invisible and voiceless: their precarious situation deprives them of documentation, hiding them from the world's eyes; the absence of adults to accompany them prevents their voices from being raised and heard. In this way, migrant children easily end up at the lowest levels of human degradation, where illegality and violence destroy the future of too many innocents, while the network of child abuse is difficult to break up'.[40]

So while states have the right to control migration and to protect the common good of the nation, this must be seen alongside the duty to resolve and regularise the situation of child migrants. It is to these principles, sitting in tension, that the UK government must continue to apply itself. The Dubs Amendment was a relatively modest proposal. In climbing down from their original commitment and thanks to the advantage of its geographic position, the UK has not responded as generously as we believe it ought.

Certainly, by comparison to the responsibility and burden taken by other countries such as Italy, Greece, Austria and Germany, the UK government has done very little.

Political pressure will continue to be needed to encourage the government to do more. In this respect, Gordon Brown's apology – cited earlier – albeit in a different but comparable context, echoes with tragic prescience, 'We are sorry that instead of caring for them, this country turned its back.'[41] The prophetic voice of the Church, especially under Pope Francis, will undoubtedly continue to provide moral leadership on the question of migration, the issue of our times. The stakes couldn't be higher in the case of children, the most vulnerable; the care of boys and girls, whether they be migrants or not, is nothing less than a biblical injunction. As we have endeavoured to show with reference to the recent debate concerning unaccompanied child migrants in the UK, Catholic Social Teaching insists that this message not only be heard but that its principles also form the basis of concrete action.

ENDNOTES

1. Passarlay, G. (2015A) 'At 13 I found sanctuary in Britain, now we're failing refugee children.' *The Guardian.* 26 October, 2015.

2. Passarlay, G. (2016B) *The Lightless Sky.* London: Atlantic Books.

3. Telephone conversation, 7 September 2017.

4. Eurostat Press Office, 'News release.' Eurostat, 11 May 2017.

5. Interview, 29 March 29 2015.

6. Passarlay, G and Khaleeli, H. 'When I fled to the UK, no one believed I was 13. Ten years on, nothing's changed.' *The Guardian,* 21 October, 2016.

7. Pope Francis. (2017) 'Message of His Holiness Pope Francis for the 104th World Day of Migrants and Refugees 2018.' The Vatican, 15 August, 2017

8. Pope Francis. (2016) 'Message of His Holiness Pope Francis for the 104th World Day of Migrants and Refugees 2017,' The Vatican, 6 September, 2016.

9. Pope Francis. (2017) 'Message of His Holiness Pope Francis for the 104th World Day of Migrants and Refugees 2018.' The Vatican, 15 August, 2017.

10. Pope Pius XII. (1952) *Exsul familia Nazarethana.* Vatican City: The Vatican.

11. Pope Paul VI. (1969) *De pastorali migratorum cura.* Vatican City: The Vatican.

12. Fumio, S. Cardinal Hamao. (2004) *Erga migrantes caritas Christi.* Vatican City, 1 May, 2004.

13. Richardson, D. (2006) 'Through a Looking Glass: Olaudah Equiano and African Experiences of the British Atlantic Slave Trade.' In Morgan, P.D. and Hawkins, S. (2006) *Black Experience and the Empire.* Oxford: Oxford University Press, p.58.

14. Hansard. (2010) 'Child Migration.' HC, 24 Feb, 2010, Column 301. Accessed at https://publications.parliament.uk/pa/cm200910/cmhansrd/cm100224/debtext/100224-0004.htm#10022460000003

15. Home Office. (2013) 'Immigration Statistics: October–December 2012, February 2013.' Accessed 5 September 2017 at https://www.gov.uk/government/publications/immigration-statistics-october-to-december-2012/immigration-statistics-october-to-december-2012#asylum-part-2-appeals-unaccompanied-asylum-seeking-children-age-disputes-and-dependants

16. Refugee Council Information. 'Children in the Asylum – August 2017.' Accessed 5 September 2017 https://www.refugeecouncil.org.uk/assets/0004/1347/Children_in_the_Asylum_System_Aug_2017.pdf

17. Ratified by the United Kingdom on 16 December 1991.

18. ZH (Tanzania) v Secretary of State for the Home Department [2011] UKSC 4; [2011] 2 A.C. 166.

19. Ibid., at para. 46.

20. British Red Cross. (2016) 'No Place for Children' Accessed 10 September 2017 at http://www.redcross.org.uk/~/media/BritishRedCross/Documents/What%20we%20do/Refugee%20support/No%20place%20for%20children.pdf

21. Hansard. (2016) 'Resettlement of unaccompanied refugee children – James Brokenshire (Minister of State for Immigration): Written statement – HCWS497.' HC, 28 January, 2016. Accessed at http://www.parliament.uk/business/publications/written-questions-answers-statements/written-statement/Commons/2016-01-28/HCWS497

22. Interview, November 21, 2016.

23. Chazan, D. (2016) 'Nearly 700 Jungle kids expected to apply for British asylum as remaining 1,600 leave Calais.' *The Telegraph*, 2 November, 2016.

24. Hansard. (2016) 'Resettlement of unaccompanied refugee children – James Brokenshire (Minister of State for Immigration):Written statement – HCWS497.' HC, 28 January, 2016. Accessed at http://www.parliament.uk/business/publications/written-questions-answers-statements/written-statement/Commons/2016-01-28/HCWS497

25. Warrell, H. and Allen, K. (2017) 'Anger as ministers shut 'Dubs' scheme to rehouse child refugees.' *Financial Times*, 8 February, 2017.

26. Siddique, H. (2017) 'Dubs delivers petition to No 10 and condemns child refugee 'cop-out'.' *The Guardian*, 11 February, 2017. Accessed at https://www.theguardian.com/world/2017/feb/11/theresa-may-under-increasing-pressure-to-restart-dubs-scheme

27. Widely reported, including in England, C. (2017) 'Lord Dubs to take on Government over deceitful child refugee U-turn.' *The Independent*, 9 February, 2017.

28. Ibid.

29. See the Red Cross response (2017) 'The Dubs Amendment and the Dublin Regulation explained' Accessed 10 September 2017 at http://www.redcross.org.uk/en/About-us/Advocacy/Refugees/Family-reunion/The-Dubs-Amendment-and-the-Dublin-Regulation-explained

30. Guillard, A. (2017) 'Refugees start to gather in Calais again, months after camp was closed.' *The Guardian*, 2 April, 2017. Accessed 20 November 2017 at https://www.theguardian.com/world/2017/apr/02/refugees-gather-calais-camp-unaccompanied-children

31. Philip, C. (2017) 'Economic migrants weaken the case of refugees, warns Lord Dubs.' *The Times*, 24 August, 2017.

32. Passarlay, G. (2016B) *The Lightless Sky*. London: Atlantic Books.

33. This has been borne out in the latest data from the European Commission 'Ninth report on relocation and resettlement' European Commission Brussels, 8.2.2017, COM(2017) 74 final.

34. House of Commons Home Affairs Committee, 'Unaccompanied Child Migrants' Thirteenth Report of Session 2016–17, March 2, 2017.

35. Hansard. (2017) 'Children: Refugees.' HL, 13 September, 2017, Vol. 783, Col 2453. Accessed at https://hansard.parliament.uk/pdf/Lords/2017-09-13

36. May, J. (2016) 'Voyage of Hope.' *The House Magazine*, 9 December, 2016, 15–17.

37. Collier, P (2016) 'The Camps don't work.' *The Spectator*, 25 March, 2017, 12–13.

38. Betts, A. and Collier, P. (2017) *Refuge: Transforming a Broken Refugee System.* London: Penguin Allen Lane.

39. Pope Francis 'Responding to Refugees and Migrants: Twenty Action Points', released August 2017 and available at https://migrants-refugees.va/documents

40. Pope Francis, 'Message of His Holiness Pope Francis for the 104th World Day of Migrants and Refugees 2018', (Vatican City, August 15, 2017).

41. Hansard 24 Feb 2010 : HC Col 301.

Conclusions

Ben Ryan

The contributions to this collection emphasise the breadth of this field. It is difficult to conduct a single debate that includes a clear answer to such disparate categories as the question of asylum for refugees on the one hand and economic workers being transferred to a new country by their company on the other. However, the question of who should be admitted to the UK (and on what terms) is settled, we will still be left with the separate, though related, question of how to integrate those migrant communities that are already present in the UK.

One thing that unites the field is that there is an opportunity for a major review and discussion. Immigration has been one of the most salient issues in British public debate since at least 2000. In fact, since 2005 it is the only issue which has ever scored higher than the economy as the most important issue to the British public.[1] There is clearly enthusiasm for solutions to the issues raised by immigration, and in a post-Brexit world there is a unique opportunity to re-assess what the UK wants from its migration policy, and the values that might underpin it.

The contributions above are a step in that direction, seeking to provoke a discussion on what a new settlement on immigration might look like with an ethical perspective.

By way of conclusion, there are four thematic issues that have arisen across the chapters that may come to define how the UK wrestles with migration in the future.

1. Identity

This answer to this critical question will have major consequences for all approaches to migration policy. Is Britishness something intrinsic, or can it be acquired? How the answer to that is formulated will significantly shape how we come to define citizenship, and the status of migrants in this country.

It has become clear that there is significant fear among a large segment of the British population that migration is changing the character of the UK and perhaps undermining British culture. This particular debate over Britishness recalls the famous Theseus' ship paradox. How many new aspects and communities can be added into the mix before the thing that is 'Britishness' ceases to be the same thing as it was 20, 50 or 100 years ago? For some, that tipping point has arrived, and only by reducing migration and more firmly asserting a British identity can solidarity be maintained.

David Goodhart's chapter is a good example of a policy that takes that aspect of solidarity and the need to protect something intrinsic about Britishness. However, it is not the only answer. It is worth noting that British immigration policy in the past has embodied the idea that Britishness does not stop at the channel. The post-war British Nationality Act of 1948 granted citizenship to subjects of Britain and the Commonwealth, for example. This has been eroded ever since, but the idea that Britishness can be extended beyond those native within the borders of Great Britain has never entirely rescinded.

These questions have grown more relevant for at least two reasons. For one thing, international levels of migration are increasing. In an era of ever advancing international transportation and globalisation, the ability to move (and to move significant distances) abroad is more readily available to a greater number of people than at any previous stage in human history. The task of integrating and navigating the challenges of an immigration level of 588,000 people in a year, more than half of whom are non-European, is always likely to be a greater challenge than the more limited (and more localised) arrivals of previous generations.

Secondly, previous efforts to extend 'Britishness' beyond the borders of the UK tended to reflect the values of the British Empire. Citizenship was conferred on the Commonwealth because those were people who had been perceived to have been in some way 'Britishised' or 'civilised' by the presence of the Empire. Previously, the context was one in which Britishness was being exported as a desirable feature, much in the same way that Christianity, the British rule of law and other marks of civilisation were being exported. The idea of Britishness was conferred upon those subjects touched by the Empire. The current post-imperial context presents a very different challenge – establishing Britishness for outsiders within the UK's own borders, rather than exporting them to other parts of the world.

Settling the question of what makes (or could make) someone British is a philosophical and ethical question that will have major policy implications. Critically, it must necessarily be that the policy work cannot take place in a moral and ethical vacuum. Developing policy before being clear on the value structure is a recipe for future confusion and conflict.

2. Responsibility

Any ethical approach to migration must naturally take seriously the question of what is owed to the vulnerable and outsiders. The question above raised the issue of solidarity and what, if anything, needs to be done to protect the UK and its people. This question looks at the other side of the equation, and the perspective of migrants.

The chapters from Anna Rowlands and Pia Jolliffe and Sam Burke look at the particular status of some of the most vulnerable migrant groups. Neither asylum seekers not child migrants make up anything like the majority of immigration into the UK, yet they are in a position of such powerlessness and vulnerability that a response on the part of the state is required. Christianity is, of course, particularly concerned with the plight of the vulnerable and outsiders, and there is a wealth of biblical and theological material on which to draw in that space (as explored in Susanna Snyder's chapter).

The use of destitution as a means of border control when it comes to asylum seekers, and the UK government's response to unaccompanied children compared to that of other European countries are both highlighted as particular instances of injustice that demand a review.

However, it is not only the most vulnerable who demand some sort of ethical response. The treatment of any migrant is an ethical issue, particularly if the policies enacted lead to negative consequences for those migrants. For example, policies aimed at economic migrants which ultimately leave migrants with fewer rights can lead to exploitation and oppression. The rights afforded to migrants, and what bodies underpin those rights against the (potentially diverging) interests of the state, need to be part of any discussion on the future of migration.

No one is advocating a scenario in which migrants are left completely devoid of rights, of course. But the question of how many rights are afforded to people in different circumstances is one which can lead to very diverging positions – as the respective essays by myself, Adrian Pabst, Susanna Snyder and David Goodhart make abundantly clear.

The corollary of rights is responsibilities – and there are equally significant debates to be had about what is to be expected of migrants. These expectations might look very different depending on the sort of migration in question. A temporary worker, present to fulfil a particular task, without any expectation of citizenship or of long-term integration, might be expected to have a different amount of responsibility, from say, a refugee, or someone seeking to obtain indefinite leave to remain in the UK. How much is expected in each case, and how to balance those responsibilities, against rights, is a fault line in much of the current debate.

3. Community

The question of the balance between the rights and responsibilities of migrants leads to a further question about how communities can live together in harmony. Critics of immigration, who would like to see levels drop significantly, or even cease entirely, still need to recognise that a great number of migrants and their descendants are already settled in the UK. Even if all migration into the UK were to stop tomorrow the issue of how to create socially cohesive communities would still be a policy concern.

Mohammed Girma's chapter points to one possible way forwards, with narrative healing being employed at a civil society level to engage a constructive way forwards that is true to the beliefs and traditions of different cultures without having to worry about being replaced, subdued or whitewashed.

Susanna Snyder goes further, arguing that encounter is a necessary part of a process of natural enrichment. The 'stranger', she argues, should not be treated simply as someone who is due some care or altruism, but rather, is someone who has something precious that builds the life of the community.

Adrian Pabst's focus on the common good, and the interconnectedness of individuals in their families and communities, likewise provides a helpful model that seeks to steer a course between liberal individualism that stresses only autonomy and a utilitarian model that strips people of their individuality for the sake of economic expediency. An approach based on common good would go some way to considering communities in the round and how individuals do not operate (or integrate) in a vacuum.

4. Humanity

A final challenge that emerges as a theme throughout several of the chapters is the risk of de-humanising migrants. All too often immigration debates are limited simply to a question of what would be best for the UK economically. In this way human existence is reduced to a matter of utility, it is stripped of personhood or any moral value.

This phenomenon is not limited to economics. Fear, and its political embodiment in security policy, can also serve to de-humanise migrants. Islamic extremism has increased a popular fear of migrants (particularly refugees) to the extent that the attitude that it is safer to take no migrants at all has taken hold of a part of the public debate. That not all migrants are Muslim, and only a tiny minority of Muslims have ever committed any such acts, is lost in an atmosphere of fear. The blanket assumptions deaden us to the humanity of individual people.

This need not lead to a simple call for open borders, or refusing to take seriously the concerns of the British people over the effects of immigration on their communities. It is, however, to call for an approach that puts humanity at its heart. This might be asserted through a stronger stance on rights, or through a recognition (as Adrian Pabst reminds us) of the fact that people exist not as atomised individuals, but in networks of relationships, or more broadly through Susanna's Snyder's focus on encounter and Mohammed Girma's on narratives.

Immigration is an issue that is hyper-emotive. Pictures of dying refugees in the Mediterranean clash in the media narrative against fears of being replaced by foreigners, benefits abuses and terrorism. At the same time, it is a highly technocratic policy area. Political debate over the intricacies of which workers ought to be allowed, or how caps ought to be calculated, seem at odds with the emotive language. This is classic example of the issue that this book has attempted to challenge.

Starting at the policy end is a mistake. Tweaking and adjusting the current system is never likely to satisfy the demands of the various sides involved in the debate. Only by first establishing the fundamental ethical basis to which we are aspiring can we build a coherent policy basis for dealing with the future of migration and the UK.

ENDNOTES

1. Migration Advisory Committee. (2016) 'December 2015, Review of Tier 2 (Executive Summary).'
2. *Briefing: UK Public Opinion toward Immigration: Overall Attitudes and Level of Concern.* Oxford: Migration Observatory.

References

Agamben, G. (1998) *Homo Sacer: Sovereign Power and Bare Life*. Stanford: Stanford University Press.

All Party Parliamentary Group on Refugees and the All Party Parliamentary Group on Migration. (2015) 'The Report of the Inquiry into the Use of Immigration Detention in the United Kingdom, March 2015'. Accessed 1 March 2017 at https://detentioninquiry.files.wordpress.com/2015/03/immigration-detention-inquiry-report.pdf

Appiah, A. (2005) *The Ethics of Identity*. Princeton: Princeton University Press.

Arendt, H. (1951) *The Origins of Totalitarianism*. San Diego, CA: Harcourt Brace Jovanovich.

Barth, K. (2004) 'The Doctrine of Reconciliation'. *Church Dogmatics*, IV.1. London: T&T Clark International.

Baum, F., MacDougall, C. and Smith, D (2006). 'Participatory action research'. *Journal of Epidemiology and Community Health*, 60, 10, 854.

Becker, S.O., Fetzer, T. and Novy, D. (2017) 'Who voted for Brexit? A comprehensive district-level analysis.' CEP Discussion Paper No 1480.

Benhabib, S. (1992) *Situating the Self: Gender, Community, and Postmodernism in Contemporary Ethics*. London: Routledge.

Bergant, D. '*Ruth: The Migrant Who Saved the People*'. In Campese, G and Ciallella, P. eds., (2003) New York: Center for Migration Studies.

Betts, A. and Collier, P. (2017) *Refuge: Transforming a Broken Refugee System.* London: Penguin Allen Lane.

Biggar, N. (2015) *Between Kin and Cosmopolis: An Ethic of the Nation.* Cambridge: James Clarke.

Bosworth, M. (2014) *Inside Immigration Detention.* Oxford: Oxford University Press.

Boyt Schell, B.A. and Schell, J.W. eds. (2008) *Clinical and Professional Reasoning in Occupational Therapy.* Baltimore: Lippincott Williams & Wilkins

Bretherton, L. (2006) 'The Duty of Care to Refugees, Christian Cosmopolitanism, and the Hallowing of Bare Life' *Studies in Christian Ethics,* 19, 1, 39–61.

British Red Cross. (2016) 'No Place for Children' Accessed 10 September 2017 at http://www.redcross.org.uk/~/media/BritishRedCross/Documents/What%20we%20do/Refugee%20support/No%20place%20for%20children.pdf

British Red Cross. (2017) 'The Dubs Amendment and the Dublin Regulation explained' Accessed 10 September 2017 at http://www.redcross.org.uk/en/About-us/Advocacy/Refugees/Family-reunion/The-Dubs-Amendment-and-the-Dublin-Regulation-explained

Brown, M. (2013) 'Migrants change UK forever: White Britons 'will be in minority by 2066.' *Daily Express,* 2 May, 2013.

Brubaker, R. (1992) *Citizenship and Nationhood in France and Germany.* Cambridge MA: Harvard University Press.

Bruggemann, W. (2001) *The Land: Place as Gift, Promise, and Challenges in Biblical Faith.* 2nd edition. Minneapolis: Augsburg.

Bruni, L. and Zamagni, S. (2016) *Civil Economy: Another Idea of the Market.* Newcastle: Agenda Publishing Ltd.

Carroll, R. (1997) 'Deportation and Disaporic Discourses in the Prophetic Literature', in Scott, J.M., ed. (1997) *Exile: Old Testament, Jewish and Christian Conceptions.* Leiden: Brill.

Castles, S. B. and Miller, M.J. (2009) *The Age of Migration: International Population Movements in the Modern World.* 4th Edition. Basingstoke: Palgrave Macmillan.

Chaplin, J. (2008) 'Beyond Multiculturalism – But To Where? Public Justice and Cultural Diversity.' *Philosophia Reformata,* 73, 2, 204.

Chazan, D. (2016) 'Nearly 700 Jungle kids expected to apply for British asylum as remaining 1,600 leave Calais.' *The Telegraph,* 2 November, 2016.

Collier, P. (2013) Oxford: Oxford University Press.

Collier, P (2016) 'The Camps don't work.', 25 March, 2017, 12–13.

Cox, Jo (2015) Maiden speech in the House of Commons, Wednesday 3 June 2015. Transcript available. Accessed 15 January at https://www.parliament.uk/business/news/2016/june/jo-cox-maiden-speech-in-the-house-of-commons

Daneshkhu, S. (2016) 'UK farms face labour shortage as migrant workers pick elsewhere.' *Financial Times*, 9 December, 2016.

Davie, G. (1994) *Religion in Britain Since 1945: Believing Without Belonging*. Oxford: Blackwell.

Dickson, J. and Eleftheriadis, P. (2012) *Philosophical Foundations of European Union Law*. Oxford: Oxford University Press.

Donaldson, L. (2010) 'The Sign of Orpah: Reading Ruth Through Native Eyes', in Kwok, P. ed. *Hope Abundant: Third World and Indigenous Women's Theology*. (2010) Maryknoll, Orbis.

El-Haj, T.R.A. (2009) 'Becoming Citizens in an Era of Globalization and Transnational Migration: Re-Imagining Citizenship as Critical Practice.' *Theory into Practice*, 48, 4, 274–282.

England, C. (2017) 'Lord Dubs to take on Government over deceitful child refugee U-turn.' *The Independent*, 9 February, 2017.

European Commission. (2017) 'Ninth report on relocation and resettlement.' European Commission Brussels, 8.2.2017, COM 74 final.

Eurostat Press Office. (2017) 'News release.' Eurostat, 11 May, 2017.

Extramiana, C. and Van Avermaet, P. (2011) 'Language requirements for adult migrants in Council of Europe member states: Report on a survey.' Strasbourg: Council of Europe, Language Policy Division.

Farisani, E. (2004) 'A Sociological Analysis of Israelites in Babylonian exile.' *Old Testament Essays*, 17, 3.

Fitzpatrick, S., Bramley, G., Sosenko, F., Blenkinsopp, J. et al. (2016) Destitution in the UK. London: Joseph Rowntree Foundation. Accessed October 2017 at https://www.jrf.org.uk/report/destitution-uk

Flanagan, R. *et al.* (2007) *TEMAS: A Multicultural Test and Its Place in an Assessment Battery*. London: Wiley Publishers.

Fox, J. (2008) *A World Survey of Religion and the State*. Cambridge: Cambridge University Press.

Freire, P. (1970) *Pedagogy of the Oppressed*. New York: Continuum.

Gibney, M. (2008) 'Asylum and the Expansion of Deportation in the United Kingdom.' *Government and Opposition*, 43, 2.

Gill, N. (2016) *Nothing Personal? Geographies of Governing and Activism in the British Asylum System*. Oxford: Wiley-Blackwell.

Goodhart, D. (2017) *The Road to Somewhere: The Populist Revolt and the Future of Politics*. London: Hurst.

Griffioen, S. (1991) 'The Metaphor of the Covenant in Habermas.' *Faith and Philosophy*, 8, 4.

Groody, D. (2009A) 'Jesus and the Undocumented Immigrant: A Spiritual Geography of a Crucified People.' *Theological Studies*, 70, 2, 298–316.

Groody, D. (2009B). 'Crossing the Divide: Foundations of a Theology of Migration and Refugees'. *Theological Studies*, 70.

Grumett, D. (2000) 'Arendt, Augustine and Evil.' *Heythrop Journal*, 41, 2, 54–169.

Guillard, A. (2017) 'Refugees start to gather in Calais again, months after camp was closed.' , 2 April, 2017. Accessed 20 November 2017 at https://www.theguardian.com/world/2017/apr/02/refugees-gather-calais-camp-unaccompanied-children

Habermas, J. (1992) *Themes in Postmetaphysical Thinking: Philosophical Essays*. Cambridge, MA: MIT Press.

Habermas, J. (2005) 'Why Europe Needs a Constitution.' *in* Eriksen, E.O., Fossum, J.E. and Menedez, A.J. eds. *Developing a Constitution for Europe*. Oxford: Routledge.

Fumio, S. Cardinal Hamao. (2004) *Erga migrantes caritas Christi*. Vatican City, 1 May, 2004.

Hansard. (2010) 'Child Migration.' HC, 24 Feb, 2010, Column 301. Accessed at https://publications.parliament.uk/pa/cm200910/cmhansrd/cm100224/debtext/100224-0004.htm#10022460000003

Hansard. (2016) 'Resettlement of unaccompanied refugee children – James Brokenshire (Minister of State for Immigration):Written statement – HCWS497.' HC, 28 January, 2016. Accessed at http://www.parliament.uk/business/publications/written-questions-answers-statements/written-statement/Commons/2016-01-28/HCWS497

Hansard. (2017) 'Children: Refugees.' HL, 13 September, 2017, Vol. 783, Col 2453. Accessed at https://hansard.parliament.uk/pdf/Lords/2017-09-13

Hardimon, M.O. (1994) *Hegel's Social Philosophy: The Project of Reconciliation*. Cambridge: Cambridge University Press.

Hegel, G.W.F. (2004) *The Philosophy of History*. Mineola, NY: Courier Dover Publications.

Heyer, K. (2012) *Kinship Across Borders: A Christian Ethic of Immigration*. Georgetown University Press.

Higgs, J. (2008) *Clinical Reasoning in the Health Professions*. 3rd edition. Philadelphia: Elsevier Health Sciences.

Hobolt, S.B. (2016) 'The Brexit vote: A Divided Nation, A Divided Continent.' *Journal of European Public Policy*, 23, 9.

Hollenbach, D. (2016) 'A Future Beyond Borders: Reimagining the Nation-State and the Church.' in Brazal, A. and Dávila, M.T. eds. *Living With(Out) Borders: Catholic Theological Ethics on the Migrations of Peoples.* Maryknoll: Orbis.

Home Office. (2005) *Controlling our Borders: Making Migration Work for Britain.* London: Home Office.

Home Office. (2013) 'Immigration Statistics: October–December 2012, February 2013.' Accessed 5 September 2017 at https://www.gov.uk/government/publications/immigration-statistics-october-to-december-2012/immigration-statistics-october-to-december-2012#asylum-part-2-appeals-unaccompanied-asylum-seeking-children-age-disputes-and-dependants

House of Commons Home Affairs Committee. (2017) 'Unaccompanied Child Migrants.', Thirteenth Report of Session 2016–17, 2 March, 2017.

Houston, F. (2015) *You Shall Love the Stranger as Yourself: The Bible, Refugees, and Asylum.* New York and Abingdon: Routledge.

Humphrey, M. (1993) 'Migrants, Workers and Refugees: The Political Economy of Population Movements in the Middle East.' *Middle East Report 181*, Radical Movements: Migrants, Workers and Refugees.

Inge, J. (2003) *A Christian Theology of Place.* Aldershot: Ashgate.

Jacobs, S. and Hai, N. (2002) 'Issues and Dilemmas.' In Anthias, F. and Lloyd, C. *Rethinking Anti-Racisms: From Theory to Practice.* London: Routledge.

Katwala, S., Rutter, J. and Ballinger, S. (2017) *Time to Get it Right: Finding Consensus on Britain's Future Immigration Policy.* London: British Future.

Kaufmann, E. and Harris, G. (2014) *Changing Places: Mapping the White Response to Ethnic Change.* London: Demos.

Kincheloe, J.L. and Steinberg, S.R. (1997) *Changing Multiculturalism.* Buckingham: Open University Press.

Kroner, R. (1971) 'Introduction to H.G.W. Hegel.' In Knox, T.M. *Early Theological Writings.* Chicago: University of Chicago Press.

Kuipers, R. (2006) 'Reconciling Shattered Modernity.' In Boeve, L. *Faith in the Enlightenment? The Critique of the Enlightenment Revisited.* Amsterdam: Rodopi.

Kukathas, C. (2003) *The Liberal Archipelago: A Theory of Diversity and Freedom.* Oxford: Oxford University Press.

Kymlicka, W. (2001) *Politics in the Vernacular: Nationalism, Multiculturalism, and Citizenship.* Oxford: Oxford University Press.

La Cocque, A. (2004) *Ruth: A Continental Commentary.* Minneapolis: Augsburg Fortress.

Levinas, E. (1985) *Totality and Infinity: An Essay on Exteriority.* Pittsburgh: Duquesne University Press.

MacIntyre, A. (1981) *After Virtue. A Study in Moral Theory*. 3rd edition. London: Duckworth.

Malkki, L. (1995) *Purity and Exile: Violence, Memory and National Cosmology among Hutu Refugees in Tanzania*. Chicago: University of Chicago Press.

Mavelli, L. and Wilson, E.K. (2017) *The Refugee Crisis and Religion: Secularism, Security and Hospitality in Question*. London: Rowman and Littlefield.

Maxwell, R. (2010) 'Evaluating Migrant Integration: Political Attitudes Across Generations in Europe.' *The International Migration Review*, 44, 1.

May, J. (2016) 'Voyage of Hope.' *The House* Magazine, 9 December, 2016, 15–17.

Meeks, W. (2003) *The First Urban Christians: The Social World of the Apostle Paul*. 2nd edition. New Haven: Yale University Press.

Migration Advisory Committee. (2016) 'December 2015, Review of Tier 2 (Executive Summary).'

Briefing: UK Public Opinion toward Immigration: Overall Attitudes and Level of Concern. Oxford: Migration Observatory.

Milanovic, B. (2016) 'There is a trade-off between citizenship and migration.' *Financial Times*, 20 April, 2016.

Milbank, J. and Pabst, A. (2016) *The Politics of Virtue: Postliberalism and the Human Future*. London: Rowman & Littlefield International.

Miller, D. (2016) *Strangers in Our Midst: The Political Philosophy of Immigration*. Cambridge, MA: Harvard University Press.

Milward, A. (2016) *The European Rescue of the Nation-State*. Oxford: Routledge.

Minh-ha, T.T. (2011) *Elsewhere, Within Here: Immigration, Refugeeism and the Boundary Event*. New York and London: Routledge.

Modood, T. (2005) *Multicultural Politics: Racism, Ethnicity and Muslims in Britain*. Edinburgh: Edinburgh University Press.

Moore, M. (2005) 'Internal Minorities and Indigenous Self-Determination.' In Eisenberg, A and Spinner-Halev, J. (2005) *Minorities Within Minorities: Equality, Rights and Diversity*. Cambridge: Cambridge University Press.

Mori, I. (1993) 'The perils of perception and the EU.' In Isasi-Diaz, A. Minneapolis: Fortress Press. Access 21 September 2017 at https://www.ipsos.com/ipsos-mori/en-uk/perils-perception-and-eu

Mori, I (2013) 'Perceptions are not reality', polls done by Ipsos Mori since 2013. Accessed 15 January 2018 at https://www.kcl.ac.uk/newsevents/news/newsrecords/2013/07-July/Perceptions-are-not-reality-the-top-10-we-get-wrong.aspx

Mountz, A. (2010) *Seeking Asylum: Human Smuggling and Bureaucracy at the Border*. Minneapolis: University of Minnesota Press.

Moxnes, H. (2003) *Putting Jesus in His Place: A Radical Vision of Household and Kingdom*. Louisville: Westminster John Knox.

Murray, D. (2017) *The Strange Death of Europe.* London: Bloomsbury.

National Council for Voluntary Organizations. (2017) 'British Social Attitudes: Record number of Brits with no religion.' London: National Centre for Social Research.

National Farmers Union. (2017) 'Access To A Competent And Flexible Workforce.' Accessed 12 September 2017 at https://www.nfuonline.com/news/eu-referendum

Nichols, V. (2001) 'The Common Good.' In Alton, D. (2001) *Citizen 21: Citizenship in the New Millennium.* London: HarperCollins Publishers Ltd.

Niles, J.D. (2010) *Homo Narrans: The Poetics and Anthropology of Oral Literature.* Philadelphia: University of Pennsylvania Press.

Nouwen, H. (1976) *Reaching Out.* Glasgow: Collins.

Novak, D. (2005) 'The Covenant In Rabbinic Thought.' In Bergant, D. (2005) *Two Faiths, One Covenant? Jewish and Christian Identity in the Presence of the Other.* Oxford: Rowman & Littlefield.

Office for National Statistics. (2015) '2011 Census analysis: Ethnicity and religion of the non-UK born population in England and Wales: 2011' 18 June, 2015.

Office for National Statistics. (2016) 'International student migration: What do the statistics tell us?' Population Briefing. January, 2016.

Office for National Statistics. (2017) 'How many people continue their stay in the UK?' 25 May, 2017.

Office for National Statistics. (2017) 'Migration statistics quarterly report:' Statistical Bulletin.

Office for National Statistics. (2017) 'Population of the UK by country of birth and nationality: 2016.' Statistical bulletin, 24 August, 2017.

Office for National Statistics. (2017) 'Migration statistics quarterly report: August 2017', 24 August, 2017.

Ogletree, T. (1985) *Hospitality to the Stranger: Dimensions of Moral Understanding.* Philadelphia: Fortress Press.

Pabst, A. (2017) 'Post-liberalism: the New Centre-ground of British Politics.' The Political Quarterly, 88, 3 July–August 2017.

Parek, B. (2000) *The Future of Multi-Ethnic Britain: Report of the Commission on the Future of Multi-Ethnic Britain.* London: Profile Books.

Passarlay, G. (2015A) 'At 13 I found sanctuary in Britain, now we're failing refugee children.' *The Guardian*, 26 October, 2015.

Passarlay, G. (2016B) *The Lightless Sky.* London: Atlantic Books.

Passarlay, G and Khaleeli, H. 'When I fled to the UK, no one believed I was 13. Ten years on, nothing's changed.' *The Guardian*, 21 October, 2016.

Philip, C. (2017) 'Economic migrants weaken the case of refugees, warns Lord Dubs.' *The Times*, 24 August, 2017.

Pole, D. (1972) 'The Concept of Reason.' In Dearden, R.F. *et al.* (1972) *Education and the Development of Reason*. London: Routledge.

Pontifical Council for Justice and Peace. (2004) Vatican City: The Vatican. Pope Francis. (2013). *Evangelii gaudium*. Vatican City: The Vatican.

Pope Francis. (2016) 'Message for the World Day of Migrants and Refugees 2016.' The Vatican, 17 January, 2016.

Pope Francis. (2016) 'Meeting with the world of labour.' The Vatican, 17 February, 2016.

Pope Francis. (2016) 'Message of His Holiness Pope Francis for the 104th World Day of Migrants and Refugees 2017,' The Vatican, 6 September, 2016.

Pope Francis. (2017) 'Message of His Holiness Pope Francis for the 104th World Day of Migrants and Refugees 2018.' The Vatican, 15 August, 2017.

Pope Francis. (2017) 'Responding to Refugees and Migrants: Twenty Action Points.' The Vatican, August 2017. Accessed at https://migrants-refugees.va/ documents

Pope Paul VI. (1965) *Gaudicum et spes*. Vatican City: The Vatican.

Pope Paul VI. (1969) *De pastorali migratorum cura*. Vatican City: The Vatican.

Pope Pius XII. (1952) *Exsul familia Nazarethana*. Vatican City: The Vatican.

Prendeville, J.G. (1972). 'The Development of the Idea of Habit in the Thought of Saint Augustine.' *Traditio*, 28.

Quijano, A. (2007) 'Coloniality and modernity/rationality.' *Cultural Studies* 21, 2–3.

Race, R. (2011) *Multiculturalism and Education*. London: Continuum.

Rawls, J. (1972) *A Theory of Justice*. Oxford: Oxford University Press.

Refugee Council Information. 'Children in the Asylum – August 2017.' Accessed 5 September 2017 https://www.refugeecouncil.org.uk/ assets/0004/1347/Children_in_the_Asylum_System_Aug_2017.pdf

'The Report of the Inquiry into the Use of Immigration Detention in the United Kingdom: A Joint Inquiry by the All Party Parliamentary Group on Refugees & the All Party Parliamentary Group on Migration.' Accessed 30 November 2017 at https://detentioninquiry.files.wordpress.com/2015/03/ immigration-detention-inquiry-report.pdf

Richardson, D. (2006) 'Through a Looking Glass: Olaudah Equiano and African Experiences of the British Atlantic Slave Trade.' In Morgan, P.D. and Hawkins, S. (2006) *Black Experience and the Empire*. Oxford: Oxford University Press.

Rieger, J. and Henkel-Rieger, R. (2016) *Unified We are a Force: How Faith and Labor Can Overcome America's Inequalities*. St Louis: Chalice Press.

Robert, H. (2011) *The Governance of Problems: Puzzling, Powering and Participation.* Bristol: Policy Press.

Rodrik, D. (2011) *The Globalization Paradox: Democracy and the Future of the World Economy.* Oxford: Oxford University Press.

Rogerson, J. (2007) *According to the Scriptures? The Challenge of Using the Bible in Social, Moral and Political Questions.* London: Equinox.

Rose, A. (2012) *Showdown in the Sonoran Desert: Religion, Law and the Immigration Controversy.* Oxford: Oxford University Press.

Rowthorn, R. (2015) *The Costs and Benefits of Large-scale Immigration.* London: Civitas.

Ruhs, M. (2013) *The Price of Rights: Regulating International Labor Migration.* Princeton, NJ: Princeton University Press.

Ruiz, J. (2011) *Readings from the Edges: The Bible and People on the Move.* Maryknoll, NY: Orbis.

Russell, F.H. (1990) "Only Something Good Can be Evil': The Genesis of Augustine's Secular Ambivalence.' *Theological Studies*, 51, 4.

Ryan, B. (2017) *A Soul for the Union.* London: Theos.

Sacks, J. (2002) *The Dignity of Difference: How to Avoid the Clash of Civilizations.* London: Continuum.

Sacks, J. (2007) *The Home We Build Together: Recreating Society.* London: Continuum.

Said, E. (2001) *Reflections on Exile and Other Essays.* London: Granta Books.

Sandel, M.J. (2009) *Justice: What's the Right Thing to Do.* London: Penguin.

Sartre, J. (1991) *The Family Idiot.* Chicago: Chicago University Press, vol. 4.

Saunders, J., Fiddian-Qasmiyeh, E. and Snyder, S. (2016) *Intersections of Religion and Migration: Issues at the Global Crossroads.* New York, NY: Palgrave.

Schmid-Scott, A. (2016) 'Reimagining violence: Hannah Arendt and the bureaucratisation of life in immigration detention.' Unlocked UK. Accessed March 2017 at http://unlocked.org.uk/blog/reimagining-violence-hannah-arendt-and-the-bureaucratisation-of-life-in-immigration-detention

The Schuman Declaration, May 9, 1950. Accessed 30 November 2017 at https://europa.eu/european-union/about-eu/symbols/europe-day/schuman-declaration_en

Shafiq, M. (1998) 'Immigration Theology in Islam.' In Timani, H., Jorgenson, A. and Hwang, A. (2015) *Strangers in this World: Multireligious Reflections on Immigration.* Minneapolis: Fortress.

Siddique, H. (2017) 'Dubs delivers petition to No 10 and condemns child refugee 'cop-out'.', 11 February, 2017. Accessed at https://www.theguardian.com/world/2017/feb/11/theresa-may-under-increasing-pressure-to-restart-dubs-scheme

Siedentop, L. (2000) *Democracy in Europe*. London, Penguin.

Smith-Christopher, D. (1996) 'Between Ezra and Isaiah: Exclusion, Transformation, and Inclusion of the 'Foreigner' in Post-Exilic Biblical Theology.' In Bret, M. (1996) *Ethnicity and the Bible*. New York: Brill.

Sniderman, P.M. and Hagendoorn, L. (2007) *When Ways of Life Collide: Multiculturalism and Its Discontents in the Netherlands*. Princeton: Princeton University Press.

Snyder, S. (2012) *Asylum-Seeking, Migration and the Church*. Abingdon: Ashgate.

Snyder, S. (2015) 'Looking through the Bars: Immigration Detention and the Ethics of Mysticism.' *Asylum-Seeking, Migration and the Church* 35, 1, 167–187.

Snyder, S., Kassam, Z. *et al.* (2013) 'Theologies and Ethics of Migration: Muslim and Christian Perspectives.' In Garnett, J. and Harris, A. *Rescripting Religion in the City: Migration and Religious Identity in the Modern Metropolis*. Farnham: Ashgate.

Sobrino, J. and Hernandez-Pico, J. (1985) *Theology of Christian Solidarity*. Maryknoll: Orbis.

Southwood, K. (2012) *Ethnicity and the Mixed Marriage Crisis in Ezra 9-10: An Anthropological Approach*. Oxford: Oxford University Press.

St. Augustine. (1961) *Confessions*. London: Penguin.

Stapleton, J. (2005) 'Citizenship versus Patriotism in Twentieth-Century England.' *The Historical Journal*, 48, 1, 151–178.

Taylor, C. (2003) *Modern Social Imaginaries*. Durham, NC: Duke University Press.

United Nations. (2016) 'International Migration Report 2015.'

United National Declaration on the Granting of Independence to Colonial Countries and Peoples. Article 2. General Assembly Resolution 1514, XV, 14 December, 1960.

Vajda, M. 'Reason and culture.' In Tymieniecka, A. (1993) *Reason, Life, Culture*. Gorinchem: Springer.

van Houten, C. (1991) 'The Alien in Israelite Law.' *JSOT Supplement Series 107*. Sheffield: JSOT/Sheffield Academic Press.

van Tubrergen, F. and Sindradóttir, J. Í. (2011) 'The Religiosity of Immigrants in Europe: A Cross-National Study.' *Journal for the Scientific Study of Religion*, 50, 2.

Volf, M. (1996) *Exclusion and Embrace: A Theological Exploration of Identity, Otherness and Reconciliation*. Nashville: Abingdon.

Wadsworth, J. *et al.* (2016) 'Brexit and the Impact of Immigration on the UK.' *CEP Brexit Analysis*, 5.

Waldon, J. (1992) 'Minority Cultures and the Cosmopolitan Alternative.' *University of Michigan Journal of Law Reform*, 751.

Warrell, H. and Allen, K. (2017) 'Anger as ministers shut 'Dubs' scheme to rehouse child refugees.' *Financial Times*, 8 February, 2017.

Weil, S. (1949) *The Need for Roots*. Oxford: Routledge.

Weil, S. (2005) 'The Iliad or the Poem of Force.' In *Simone Weil: An Anthology*. London: Penguin.

Wells, S. (2006) *God's Companions: Reimagining Christian Ethics*. Oxford: Wiley-Blackwell.

Williams, R. (2015) 'Insubstantial Evil.' In *On Augustine*. London: Bloomsbury.

Wilsher, D. (2012) *Immigration Detention: Immigration Detention: Law, History, Politics*. Cambridge: Cambridge University Press.

Wodak, R. (1996) *The Politics of Fear: What Right-wing Populist Discourses Mean*. London: Sage.

Wogaman, J.P. and Strong, D. (1996) *Readings in Christian Ethics: A Historical Sourcebook*. Louisville: Westminster John Knox.

Zabala, S. (2017) 'How to be a European (Union) Philosopher.', 23 February, 2017. Accessed 15 May 2017 at https://opinionator.blogs.nytimes.com/2012/02/23/how-to-be-a-european-union-philosopher

Contributor Biographies

Br **Samuel Burke** OP is a Deacon and a former practicing Barrister who is currently undertaking legal research and teaching in Oxford, when he is not studying theology in Rome.

David Goodhart is a journalist, author and think tanker – currently head of the demography unit at the Policy Exchange think tank. He is the founder and former editor of *Prospect* magazine and the former director of the centre-left think tank Demos. His book was runner up for the Orwell book prize. In his new book (a bestseller) Goodhart identifies the value divisions in British society that help to explain the Brexit vote and the rise of populism.

Pia Jolliffe is a Research Scholar at the Las Casas Institute for Social Justice, and a Teaching and Research Associate at the Nissan Institute of Japanese Studies, University of Oxford. She is author of several peer-reviewed articles and monographs, including *Learning, Migration and Intergenerational Relations. The Karen and the Gift of Education* (2016, Palgrave Macmillan).

Mohammed Girma is an International Advocacy Officer (IBAC), Visiting Lecturer of Intercultural Studies at London School of Theology and Research Associate at the University of Pretoria. Girma is the author of Understanding Religion and Social Change in Ethiopia (Palgrave Macmillan 2012) and co-editor of two volumes Democracy, Conflict and the Bible (Bible Society, 2015); and Christian Citizenship in the Middle East (JKP, 2017). Currently, Girma is editing The Healing of Memories: African Christian Responses to Politically Induced Trauma (Rowan & Littlefield, 2018).

Adrian Pabst is Reader in Politics in the School of Politics and International Relations at the University of Kent, UK, where he also directs the Centre for Federal Studies. His research is at the interface of political thought, political economy, ethics and religion. He is the co-editor of *Blue Labour: Forging a New Politics* (2015) and the co-author (together with John Milbank) of *The Politics of Virtue: Post-liberalism and the Human Future* (2016). He is a contributor to *The New Statesman*, *The Guardian*, Comment is Free, *ABC Religion and Ethics, International Herald Tribune*, (now *International New York Times*) and *The Conversation*. Currently he is writing a book on alternatives to liberal democracy and leading a project with the St Paul's Institute on reforming free movement of capital and labour.

Anna Rowlands is a political theologian and the St Hilda Associate Professor of Catholic Social Thought and Practice at the University of Durham. She is also the Deputy Director of the Centre for Catholic Studies, University of Durham, and the founding chair of a national network that brings together academics and practitioners in the arena of Catholic Social Thought and practice. She has worked on theological ethics and migration for the last decade and is currently a researcher on the AHRC/ERSC funded project Refugee Hosts (www.refugeehosts. org). She has worked closely with Citizens UK, Jesuit Refugee

Service and various Caritas agencies on migration matters. She is the author of forthcoming *Catholic Social Teaching: A Guide for the Perplexed* (2018, Bloomsbury) and co-editor of *T&T Clark Reader in Political Theology* (2018, Bloomsbury).

Ben Ryan is a researcher at Theos, the religion and society think tank. He holds degrees in Theology from the University of Cambridge and in European Politics from the LSE. He is the author of a number of reports including *A Soul for the Union* (2016, Theos) and *Christianity and Mental Health: Theology, Activities, Potential* (2017, Theos).

Susannah Snyder is Assistant Director at Catherine of Siena College, and Tutor in Theology at the University of Roehampton. She is also a Research Associate at the Oxford Centre for Christianity and Culture at Regent's Park College, Oxford, and an Associate Member of the Faculty of Theology and Religion, University of Oxford. She is the author of *Asylum Seeking Migration and Church* (2012, Ashgate), the co-editor of *Church in an Age of Global Migration: A Moving Body* (2015, Palgrave) and *Intersections of Religion and Migration: Issues at the Global Crossroads* (2016, Palgrave).

Subject Index

Author Index